Negotiation by Peaceful Means

Nepo-India Territorial Disputes

By Bishnu Pathak, Ph.D.

Susmita Bastola, Ph.D. Candidate

Published by Cook Communication

1407 Getzelman Drive

Elgin, IL 60123

www.author-me.com

Not affiliated with Cook Communication Ministries

Cover Art - Ms. Susmita Bastola

National Library of USA Cataloguing in Publication

ISBN

978-1-387-79689-2
Imprint: Lulu.com

Imprint: Lulu.com

Printed and bound in the USA

Negotiation by Peaceful Means
Nepo-India Territorial Disputes

Table of Contents

"Asato mā sadgamaya; tamasomā jyotirgamaya; mrityormāamritam gamaya; Oṁ śhānti śhānti śhāntiḥ (Lead me from the unreal to the real, lead me from darkness to light; lead me from death to immortality, Oṁ peace, peace, peace)"

- Veda, Bṛihadāraṇyaka Upaniṣad
(1.3.28.)

Abstract

Nepo is a prefix designation of Nepal. The territorial dispute is contention between Nepal and India. This study is a review of entire historical treaties, agreements, and documents on disputed Kalapani areas. And it connects with individuals/institutions motivating for change acknowledged by signing negotiation through dialogical means. Its objectives are four-fold: (i) to examine the Nepo-India territorial disputes; (ii) to gather testimonies and other witnesses; (iii) to listen to the voices of commoners, civil society, experts, and leaders of both nations; and (iv) to ease the dialogue process for negotiation. The lessons learned-centric approach inspired the authors to undertake this study The paper is prepared based on archival research with the first author's over 100 international publications tracking snow-ball techniques. There are several testimonies collected on the disputes. First, British-India unilaterally drafted the Sugauli Treaty in 1816. Nepal sent junior officials to sign the Treaty in 94 days, ignoring British-India's ultimatum for 15 days. Moreover, as the attack on the capital of Nepal had been on the door, the Government was forced to agree to the Treaty. Second, Nepal lost about 40 percent of its territories due to the Treaty. Third, the Nepo-India Joint Committee (JTBC) was set up in November 1981 to re-establish and reconstruct the boundary lines to keep the borders intact. Fourth, while Indian PM I.K. Gujral had undertaken a State Visit to Nepal in June 1997, he directed the JTBC to resolve the territorial disputes. Further, he vowed to withdraw his army from Kalapani if the report concluded that Kalapani areas belong to Nepal. Fifth, while Jaswant Singh, the Indian Foreign Minister was visiting Kathmandu in 1999, a Joint Communiqué was issued mentioning the disputed territories and instructing the JTBC clearly to demarcate Kalapani areas. In 26 years, the JTBC outlined 98 percent boundary lines excluding Kalapani areas. Sixth, the EPG was formed in January 2016 to review bilateral treaties and agreements, replace the 1950 Peace Treaty, and combat terrorism. In 30-months, the EPG had prepared a single report by consensus, but PM Modi denied to accept the report. Seventh, the Arrowsmith published a Nepo-India map from London in January 1816 which identifies the Kali

River originating from Limpiyadhura instead of the artificial Kali River constructed in front of the temple in Kalapani. Eighth, Bhairab Risal (a 93 years old former Civil Servant) conducted the Population Census in Limpiyadhura villages in 1961, east of Kali River. Ninth, the Land Administration Office, Doti district has gathered testimonies of receipts from Limpiyadhura villagers. Lastly, after Peace Accord in 2006, 11 Prime Ministers including a monarch have already been appointed in Nepal, but none of them have raised questions over the disputed territories. This happened as all leaders competed for India's blessings to attain State Power. India isolates itself in this region because of its focus on jingoistic mediaism against the poor and weak neighbouring counties, putting low priority on holding dialogue and mitigating differences for negotiation. India has territorial disputes with all the adjoining neighbours. There is a fault of Nepali leaders too. Many Nepalese communist leaders have double standard characteristics to advocate on behalf of China during the day and be pro-Indian and pro-American at night. There is urgency for India to sort out the fault lines in its (controlled) democracy.

Keywords: Dialogue, Negotiation, *Nepo*-India, Territorial Disputes, Kalapani, Limpiyadhura, Lipulek, treaty, and Sugauli Treaty.

Prologue

Authors Bishnu Pathak and Susmita Bastola deserve highest marks for this historical account of a key territorial dispute. Any reader must react with amazement while witnessing one-time agreements and repeated broken promises as Nepal's powerful neighbors have fought with each other, each desiring a larger piece of this beautiful and powerless country.

Here, ignoring the lessons of colonialism, these countries hassle with each other to achieve influence and territory along a mighty river. Reading along, the history nearly screams with the fact that neither neighboring country shows humanitarian concern for the country of Nepal and the residents who live along the forever-disputed, border.

Amazing, too, the unconcern each powerful neighbor seems to show for past agreements, each pointing to its own advantage in controlling this invaluable portion of Nepal.

In this book, Bishnu Pathak and Susmita Bastola carefully and sympathetically document the history of these negotiations, showing how neither of the two neighboring parties to this territorial can seem to ever come to meaningful agreement.

The impeccable scholarly work of these authors is commendable and is a testament to the trustworthiness of their unique account.

May the leaders of China, India, and Nepal read this book and agree to follow the authors' proven Three-Dialogue

Track approach to resolving major disputes. May this vital volume lead to a successful resolution of this dispute, and — for perhaps the first time in history — produce an agreement which will take into account the people of the disputed territory.

---Bruce L. Cook, Ph.D.

Vice President/Co-Founder

Worldwide Peace Organization

Preface

This book is an account of the reviews of historical documents and treaties related to the Kalapani disputed areas that lie between Nepo-India and proposes peaceful dialogues among the civilians to the leaders and executive authority of both countries.

Territorial disputes are not a new phenomenon in the world. Historically, the common causes of war or conflict have been conducted because of territorial disputes. Since World War II, Asian countries have been prone to decolonization and maintaining their domination in foreign territories with the neighboring countries. India is the one undergoing several territorial disputes with its neighboring countries, for instance, Jambu-Kashmir with Pakistan, Ladhak with China, and Kalapani with Nepal. India settled the territorial disputes with both adjoining countries Bhutan and Bangladesh by peaceful means and Nepal hopes to receive the same dispute transformation by adapting the informal-indirect and formal-direct dialogue tracks method.

Nepal, a small, sandwiched, and landlocked Himalayan country's domestic politics and economy have been undergoing several turbulences, instability, and shifts. India has been criticized by the Nepalese people for its insensitive media responses, simply called jingoistic mediaism after the earthquake and the promulgation of the Republican Constitution, 2015. After the publication of a new territorial map of India including the Kalapani areas, anti-Indian sentiments have largely prevailed among the greater Nepalese populace.

They began to pressurize the political parties and the Nepalese Government too. The government of Nepal also published the new map, including the Kalapani areas, by sending diplomatic notes on several occasions to the Government of India. Despite officially responding to the diplomatic notes, Indian media was insensitive to the people and leaders of Nepal and spread fake news. The media's jingoism was largely practiced both on land and abroad, spreading anti-Nepalese and anti-Chinese sentiment among the masses. With the spreading of exaggerated jingoism stating 'Nepal is in the fold of China', Nepalese people further turned against the Government of India, its controlled politics, and its fake 'might is right' propaganda.

The second half of this book offers an exclusive dialogic pyramid model to resolve or transform the Nepo-India territorial disputes. Nepal and India are not only territorially close, but they are enjoying excellent connections of history, culture, religion, and tradition engagement from people to people. Therefore, dialogue at the bottom level can equally serve as a peaceful means to solve territorial disputes. The bottom-up dialogue approach among the civilians can transform anti-national sentiments and media jingoism. Ultimately, both countries love the cultural ties-up by maintaining peace, coexistence, and harmony.

There has been a self-admiration that India is the world's largest democratic country. But the question is, why does India not sit for a dialogue with Nepal to transform the territorial disputes by peaceful means? Both nations should open the channels for informal-indirect and formal-direct dialogue and participation among state-to-state and non-state to non-state actors, grassroots people, civil society, and religious leaders. Dialogue begets the negotiation to transform the disputes by peaceful means.

Professor Bishnu Pathak, Ph.D. (Nepal)

Susmita Bastola, Ph.D. Candidate (Japan)

July 11, 2022

1. Introduction

Nepo is a linguistic and ethnological term. Nepo is a prefix designation of Nepal (Pathak, 2015). Nepo has unique customs, distinctive traditional heritages and rich cultural features. Its customs articulate from Hindu-Buddhist traditions, civilizations, and societies. Nepo cultures encompass diversities along with 125th distinct ethnic, tribal, racial, and social groups which exist with their own religions and beliefs in varied regions such as Tarai-Madhes, Hills and Mountains. It has its own distinctive cultural rites, rituals, music, songs, dances and cuisines. It connects with explicit identity among the inhabitants of the territorial values.

Territorial is an area of land under the jurisdiction of a concerned State (Territory- Laxico.com). According to International Politics, territory is the total area in which a state may extract power for resources (Hickman, 2016). It is a politico-administrative division under control of the nation. Dispute is (dis)agreeing with what someone acts or says. It is an argument or disagreement between individuals or groups (Dispute- Collinsdictionary.com). Christoph Ashreuer says, "A dispute is a denied in order to contest the jurisdiction of international court or tribunal" (undated). Dispute is a conflict or controversy in which a demand on one side is met by contrary claims on the other

(Dispute-thelawdictionary.com). Dispute generally happens owing to emergence of a contentious issue.

A territorial dispute occurs when the Government representative of one country releases clear statement(s) claiming sovereignty and integrity over a specific portion of territory administered by another country (Mitchell, May 26, 2016). It defines an explicit contention between two or more nation-states concerning dominion over a specific piece of terrestrial territory. There are over 800 territorial disputes which have occurred internationally since 1816 (Hensel, Paul R. 2000) in Table 1, whereas Nepal had signed the most controversial Sugauli Treaty with British Indian in 1816 (Annex – I).

Table 1: Territorial disputes around the world (1816-2001)			
#	Region	Status	Number of claims
1	Western Hemisph -eres	All data collection completed (1816-2001)	82 claimed territories (128 dyadic claims/19 on-going)
2	Europe	Main data collection completed (1816-2001), including West European peaceful settlement attempts;	96 claimed territories (238 dyadic claims/10

		East European peaceful attempts nearly completed	ongoing)
3	Africa	Main data collection completed (1816-2001), peaceful settlement attempt research underway	76 claimed territories (161 dyadic claims/22 ongoing)
4	Middle East	Main data collection completed (1816-2001), peaceful settlement attempts nearly completed	42 claimed territories (95 dyadic claims/5 ongoing)
5	Asia and Oceania	Main data collection completed (1816-2001), peaceful settlement attempt research underway	76 claimed territories (215 dyadic claims/53 ongoing)
6	Entire world		372 claimed territories (837 dyadic claims/109 ongoing)
Source: https://www.paulhensel.org/icowterr.html			

Territorial disputes occur from sovereign states to dependent territories, i.e., Pyrenean countries, developing to the developed world. Some disputes are long simmering like Jammu-Kashmir, but boiling points such as Crimea (Conant, March 6, 2014) and Taiwan Strait (Bush, 2006). A few are Ladakh, Golan Heights, West Bank, East China Sea, and Kalapani area.

Many books have overviewed the territorial disputes which were often caused by armed conflict or war. Allan J. Day covered a total of 80 contemporary borders and territorial disputes in the world (November 16, 1987). Kalevi J Holsti presented data on wars (1991). Paul K. Huth developed a theory of territorial disputes (1996). Paul R. Hensel reviewed the literature on territorial disputes and wars (2000). Harvey Starr presented spatial features of border disputes (2005). Sara McLaughlin Mitchell and Paul R. Hensel overviewed the data of disputes (2010). Monica Duffy Toft summarized the literature on territorial disputes, civil wars, and interstate conflicts (2014).

On May 8, 2020, Indian Defense Minister, Rajnath Singh, inaugurated an 80 km (50 miles) newly constructed Lipulek Pass (Ethirajan, June 10, 2020) link road to Mt. Kailash Mansarovar for the Hindu pilgrims. The territorial disputes intensified between the two great neighbors as Nepal claims Kalapani, Lipulek, and Limpiyadhura are their territory. As a result, Nepal has published a new political map including Kalapani areas endorsed by both Federal Parliaments. A great majority of conscious people of both nations pressed the Governments of both nations to resolve the problems through dialogue and negotiation.

4

India fears holding dialogue and negotiation due to the lack of historical facts, evidence, and testimonies.

Territorial disputes lead to several types of diplomatic arguments including boundary, river, maritime, identity, economic, and cultural, among other issues. This study focuses more on the adjoining border dispute of the Kalapani areas, initiated by India on November 2, 2019 (Giri, November 4, 2019) administrating a new cartographic map that created anti-India sentiments in Nepal (Nayak, 2012). It means, it helped further to enhance Nepo-India territorial dispute. Territorial dispute changes the personal (feeling or perception), relational (person-person, group-person, group to group), structural (international, political, and legal), and socio-cultural (values and identities) of attitudinal behavior.

Testimony is proof and demonstration of some facts and evidence (Testimony-etymonline.com). It is a formal statement about something given in a court of law (Testimony- dictionary.cambridge.org). Testimony is the statement and or declaration of a witness under oath, usually in court (Testimony-dictionary.com). Testimony is a form of facts or evidence. It is a formal spoken or written statement and witness (third-party) of truth.

Negotiation is an interaction and process between parties who compromise to agree on matters of mutual interest (Adnan et al, August 2016). Bill Scott says, "A negotiation is a form of meeting between the parties" (November 1981). Negotiation is a process in which two or more entities exchange goods or services (Wall and Blum, June 1, 1991). Negotiation is the matter of bargaining process in which two disputing (Nepo-India) parties mutually reach an agreement accepting terms of one another.

The General Objective of the study thoroughly reviews the entire historical treaties, agreements, and protocols that were signed by both nations and the trends of their compliance. The Specific Objectives are to examine the existing situations of Nepo-India territorial disputes; to find out the entire historical facts and evidence; to listen to the voices of commoners, civil society, intellectuals, and leaders of both countries, and to ease the dialogue process for negotiation.

The first author's reflections are gained either through literature review or exchanging and sharing approach rather than theoretical conception. Therefore, this state-of-the-art paper is pursued based on archival research with a lessons-learned-centric approach following the networking tracking method or snowball techniques. The pioneer Chapter assists to initiate informal and indirect (back-channel) and formal and direct (front-channel) dialogue on Nepo-India existing boundary line problems on the course to resolve the disputes permanently through negotiation by peaceful means.

2. Territorial Disputes Testimonies

Nepal and India are locked in a historic, diplomatic, socio-cultural, cartographic, economic, and to some extent, political assistance or participation. Nepal claims that India has encroached on 78 territories of Nepalese land whereas Nepal has occupied 17 places of India. The 1,240 (15.5%) of the total 8,000 boundary pillars along the Nepo-India border have been missing (Basnyat, November 25, 2019). However, the Nepalese Armed Police Force (APF) Chhinnamasta Brigade stated that there are 4,027 pillars along the border in which 2,064 (51%) border pillars are intact, 704 (17%) need repair, 319 (8%) need replacement, 91 (2%) were washed away by rivers, and 849 (21%) have been missing in the province in 464 km in border (Napali Sansar, June 29, 2021).

Out of them, the dispute generally occurs over the ownership of 335 sq. km. of land called the Kalapani area near Nepal's western tri-junction border with India and China (Muni, May 22, 2020). It has not yet outlined the origination of the Mahakali River, but the Treaty of Sugauli mentions, "Kali is the western border of Nepal with India" (Roy Chowdhury, June 13, 2020).

The Kalapani areas were focused largely on the establishment of Indian military posts. Nepal virtually overlooked the Kalapani area situating military posts from 1961 to 1997. In September 1998, the Communist Party of Nepal (Marxist-Leninist), Nepali Congress, and the Rashtriya Prajatantra Party coalition Government reached an agreement on disputed border areas and raised some concerns about dialogues for bilateral negotiation. The agreed points were: first, all border disputes, including Kalapani, will be resolved through mutual talks with India; second, these talks will also incorporate a discussion of the 1950 Nepo-India security treaty (Peace and Friendship Treaty); and third, the NC-UML Government will prepare a report on the Mahakali Treaty and distribution of hydropower and water resources in their border areas (Rose, 1999). The forthcoming Nepo-India Transit Treaty, which may be held in early 1999, shall try to incorporate most of the disputed points with New Delhi. However, the disputed issues could not be raised with India as expected.

Deputy Prime Minister Bamdev Gautam raised a question of control over the Kalapani area by India while the then Prime Minister I.K. Gujral had been on a three-day State Visit to Nepal from June 5-7, 1997 (Dhungel & Pun, 2009). Gujral agreed the existing Nepo-India territorial disputes would be resolved (Prakash, May 22, 2020, & Parashar, May 19, 2020) through the Joint Working Group, named Joint Technical Level Nepal-India Boundary Committee (JTLNIBC). He further stated that, if the Committee report concluded that the Kalapani area belongs to Nepal, India will withdraw the army from there immediately.

The JTLNIBC (JTBC) establishment was agreed upon on February 25, 1981, and was finally set up in November 1981 for the purpose of re-establishing and reconstructing the boundary pillars that were found lost; recording the encroachment along the boundary called *dashgaja* (No-man's land), and asking to manage and keep the boundary clean and to prepare the modality for periodic inspection to keep the boundary intact. The JTLINBC worked for 26 years to maintain the Nepo-India boundary line intact after carefully surveying with deliberations and extensions. The Committee outlined 98 percent boundary lines excluding Kalapani and Susta before it was dissolved in January 2008 (Baral, December 2019). The remaining 2 percent of the boundary lines work on 37 km. comprises barren snow-covered rocks including Kalapani (17 km.) and lowlands Susta (20 km.) owing to differences in opinions of Indian authorities, and other basic materials. The JTBC prepared 182 sheets of strip maps of their border, excluding disputed areas of Susta and Kalapani (Giri, May 11, 2020). Regrettably, neither country ratified the maps, but India again urged Nepal to endorse the maps, stating that Kalapani and Susta disputes shall be resolved in the due course.

On September 11, 1999, while Jaswant Singh, Indian External Affairs Minister, was visiting Kathmandu, a Joint

Communiqué was issued mentioning the problem of Kalapani areas. They instructed the Joint Technical Committee to analyze the historical facts and testimonies efficiently for the demarcation of the western sectors, including the area of Kalapani, and were directed to complete their works on time (Thapa, December 2010). The JTBC used boundary maps based on Sugauli Treaty which were accepted by both countries.

The JTBC could not materialize the works on time because of India's divergent opinions on border demarcations and disputes on certain segments. Even though, the dispute with China on Sagarmatha was settled through dialogue and ended while the visiting Prime Minister Chou En-Lai made a statement in Kathmandu on April 28, 1960, that "Sagarmatha belongs to Nepal" (Shrestha, January 17, 2010).

The Nepo-India dispute was triggered on November 2, 2019, when a new Official Politico-Administrative map was issued by India's Home Ministry changing the status of Jammu and Kashmir into a Union Territory. Similarly, the Kalapani area was also included in the map; it created a ruckus in Nepal (Dixit & Dhakal, May 19, 2020). The inclusion of Nepal's Kalapani, Lipulek Pass, and Limpiyadhura areas into the map resulted in the wave of protests in all tiers - central, provincial, and local levels – against India. Nepal asked for Foreign Secretary-level talks sending three notes on November 20, 22, and December 30, 2019, but Kathmandu got no response from India (Mehta, June 26, 2020). When the offending map issue was simmering, Nepal became furious when Defense Minister Rajnath Singh virtually inaugurated a link road connecting the border with China, at the Lipulek Pass (Xavier, June 11, 2020). The connectivity of the road was aimed at strengthening India's defense supply lines and facilitating smooth passage for pilgrims to Kailash Mansarovar (Muni, May 22, 2020). Nepal claims that Kalapani, Limpiyadhura, and Lipulek Pass are the territories of Nepal lying in the Darchula district (Giri, May 8, 2020, & Thapa, May 13, 2020).

On May 15, 2015, Indian Prime Minister Narendra Modi and His counterpart Li Keqiang of China agreed to expand border trade through the Lipulek Pass in Beijing. The 28th point of the Joint Communiqué agreed to hold negotiations on the course to expand the border trade at the Lipulek Pass. The Communiqué states,

> "The two sides recognized that enhancing border areas cooperation through border trade, pilgrimage by people of the two countries and other exchanges can effectively promote mutual trust, and agreed to further broaden this cooperation so as to transform the border into a bridge of cooperation and exchanges. The two sides agreed to hold negotiations on augmenting the list of traded commodities and

expand border trade at Nathu La, Qiangla/Lipu-
Lekh Pass, and Shipki La".

(Press Information Bureau Government of India,
May 15, 2015).

As Nepal claims Lipulek to be a part of its territory, a far
western part of Nepal, both India and China needed to
attain Nepal's consent to expand their border trade. On
May 15, 2015, the Communist Party of India (Marxist)
leader Sitaram Yechury denounced the Joint Communiqué
of China and India stating that both countries should have
consulted Nepal before deciding on the trade to Tibet and
connectivity plan to Mansarovar (The Kathmandu Post,
June 11, 2015).

The Lipulek Pass is located at the Nepo-China borderline
which is an ancient route for merchants and pilgrims
transiting between Nepal and Tibet, China. During the Sino-
India war (October 20-November 21, 1962) (Hoffmann,
1990), Chinese military forces chased away the Indian
military forces up to the Lipulek Pass and retreated. The
Indian military had already realized Lipulek Pass as a
potential strategic security point and established their
check-posts. Instead of withdrawing its forces from there,
India has been increasing its official numbers as well as
strengthening its infrastructures one after another day.

The territory characterizes part of the basin of the Kalapani River at an altitude of 3600–5200 meters. Lipulek lies at the top of the valley of Kalapani which is a traditional trading route for Bhotiyas, Tibet of Kumaon, and the Tinker valley of Nepal (Manzardo, Dahal & Rai, Undated). As the Lipulek Pass is a strategically important place to watch both China and Nepal, the Indian Army has taken control of the area. Even though Nepal has been claiming that Lipulek, Kalapani, and Limpiyadhura are parts of its since 1997, India has always turned deaf ears.

Besides, the Kalapani area has been a crucial security point in which a constructed road connects the Lipulek Pass, but India claims that Lipulek Pass lies in the Pithoragarh district of (Uttarakhand) at the height of 17,000 feet. Mansarovar is around 90 km from Lipulek Pass (PTI, May 8, 2020). A vehicle can go on a 5-km trek inside China across Lipulek. Thus, the 5 days of travel were then reduced to two days of road travel (Santhanam, August 12, 2019). The Indo-China Agreement of 1954 mentioned Lipulek for Indo-Tibetan trade (Nayak, June 9, 2015) and Kailash-Mansarovar pilgrimage traffic that was reaffirmed in another Trade Agreement in 2015.

The Sino-India trade agreement was signed on April 29, 1954, in which traders and pilgrims of both countries shall travel through Shipki-La Pass and Lipulek Pass (Nayak, June 9, 2015). The 1962 Sino-India War ended trading with China through Lipulek Pass. When Prime Minister Rajiv Gandhi visited Beijing in December 1988, Sino-India relations continued to improve trade (Hsin-Chi and Brosseau, 1991). A memorandum of understanding on Resumption of Border Trade was signed on December 13, 1991, during Premier Li Peng's visit to New Delhi, and the border Protocol was signed on July 1, 1992 (Ministry of Foreign Affairs, June 23, 2003). Both Resumption of Border and Protocol of Entry and Exit Procedure agreements mutually recognized Lipulek Pass as a border trading point (Chaudhary, June 1, 2020). Again, on April 11, 2005, the Chinese Premier, Wen Jiabao and Indian PM Manmohan Singh signed an agreement aiming at confidence-building along the Line of Actual Control, Article V of which stated: "Both sides agree in principle to expand the mechanism of border meeting points to include Kibithu-Damai in the Eastern Sector and Lipulek Pass/Qiang La in the Middle Sector. The precise locations of these border meeting points will be decided through mutual consultations" (Cowan, December 14, 2015).

On February 4, 1817, the Acting Chief Secretary John Adams of the East India Company sent an order letter to the G.W. Trail the Commissioner of Kumaon along with a copy letter to Edward Gardner, the Resident Commissioner of British India in Kathmandu. The letter instructed the surrender of the eastern side of the Kali as per the spirit of the Treaty to the Government of Nepal, for details of which are mentioned in the Box I.

Box - I

To,

The Honourable

Edward Gardner

Resident at

Catmandhoo

Sir;

I am directed to acknowledge of receipt of your dispatch of the 12th Ultimos, enclosing of your letter to the Resident of the Lucknow, respecting a spot of on the left bank of Gogra which Chautrea Bum Sah is anxious, should be left within the Nipaulese Frontier, and responding for the consideration and order of the Government a claim prepared by the Chautrea to that portion of the Pergunnah of Beasse (Byaus), which lies East of Kali and which is at present in the occupation of the British Government, as an appendage of the Province of Kumaon.

The tenor of your letter to the Resident of Lucknow is entirely approved.

With respect to the Bum Sah's claim to the track of the eastern side of the Kali, the Governor-General of the Council is of opinion, that according to the Letter of the Treaty, the Government of Nipaul is entitled of the restoration of it, notwithstanding its hitherto having been regarded as annexed to the British Province of Kumaon. I am accordingly directed to intimate to you that the Acting Commissioner for Kumaon will be instructed to surrender it to the officers of the Nipaulese Government.

His Lordship of Council approves at the same time of the caution observed by you in declining to take any steps at the instance of the Nipaulese Minister on this affair until you have referred the question for the decision of your Government and should receive its order.

Fort William	I have the honour to be Sir
4th February 1817	Yours must Obedient
	Humble Servant
	John Adam
	Acting Chief Secretary to the
	Government

(Source: Manandhar, Mangal Siddhi & Hriday Lal Koirala. (2001, June). "Nepal-India Boundary: River Kali as International Boundary". *Tribhuvan University Journal*. Volume XXIII, No. 1).

Almost a month later (March 2, 1817), John Adams directed to the G. W. Trall Esq., Acting Commissioner at Kumaon, to acknowledge the receipt of all lands, for return, situated to the Eastward of the Kali (see, Box - II).

On March 8, 1817, Kumaon Commissioner stated that they were then informed that the villages situated east of Kali are now [to] be attached to the Pergunnah of Dotee [Nepal]. Besides, Tinkar and Changroo villages, the remaining six villages: Boodhe [Budhi], Gurbhuyan [Garbyang], Goonjee, Nabhee, Okutee [Nihal?] and Kuthee [Kuti] had been parts of Nepal. The Zamindars resided on the west side of Kali in British India, and their tenants lived on the east of the Kali River in Nepal. The Zamindars, thus, lost six villages (Dhungel and Pun, August 2014).

Box - II

G. W. Traill Esq.

Acting Commissioner at Kumaon

Dear Sir;

I am directed to acknowledge the receipt of your dispatch of 8th instant related to the villages of Pergunnah Byaus situated to the Eastward of the Kali and enclosing a petition from the Booteea Zimeendars of that Pergunnah.

The letter and spirit of the Treaty for Peace give the Nipaulese Government the un-doubtable rights to all lands situated to the Eastward of the Kali, and whether

---

here to fore forming part of the province of Kumaon or not and on the other hand it is extremely undesirable to manifest any reluctance to give prompt and full effect to those situations of the Treaty by which the extent of the remaining possessions of the Nipaulese is defined. There is litter reason to support that the Nipaulese Government would consent to the relinquish the land in question for a precursory payment and on the whole, the Governor-General in Council has determined to proceed at once to the restoration of Nipaulese villages and lands in question, which you will accordingly be prepared to makeover to the officers of that Government on their application.

In reply to the petition of the Booteea Zimeendars, you will be pleased to explain to them the necessity of adhering to the conditions of the Treaty which all lands situated Eastward of the Kali River were secured to the Nipaulese and that the occupation of the Villages and lands of Pergunnah Byaus on that side of the river, having taken place under an erroneous view of the questions, they must now be transferred to the Nipaulese, however desirous, the British Government may be to retain under its own away from the Zimeendars and Inhabitants of those Villages.

With regards to the annual depredation stated to be committed in the Province of the Kumaon by the

Inhabitants of the Goorkah Pergunnah of Joomlee, I am directed to desire that you will report more, particularly on that subject, in order to that such representation as may be deemed proper may be made to the Government of Nipaul with a view to present the renewal of those outrages.

A copy of your letter of this dispatch will be transmitted to the Resident at Catmandhoo.

Fort William	I have the honour to be
The 2nd March 1817	John Adam
	Acting Chief Secretary to the Government

(Source: Manandhar, Mangal Siddhi & Hriday Lal Koirala. (2001, June). "Nepal-India Boundary: River Kali as International Boundary". *Tribhuvan University Journal*. Volume XXIII, No. 1).

The Sugauli Treaty had given territorial concessions in which many parts of Nepalese lands were delivered to British India. It allowed Britain to recruit Nepali in the name of Gorkhas for military services (Sharda, Undated) that still recruit in small numbers. The forceful signature of Sugauli Treaty, Nepal lost about 40 percent of its territories, including Darjeeling, Sikkim, west of Kali River like Kumaon, Garhwal (Uttarakhanda), some territories to the west of Sutlej River (Himanchal Pradesh) and many Tarai, lowlands of Nepal. Similar meals, formal dresses, festivals, and death-marriage ceremonies and Nepali speaking castes and ethnicities are still found in Nepal's lost territories.

Even though Junga Bahadur Rana assisted British India in soldiers revolution, the East India Company happily returned the western Tarai which is known as *Naya Muluk* (new state): Banke, Bardiya, Kailali and Kanchapur districts to Nepal on Kartik 3, 1917 BS (November 1, 1860 AD) through a Supplementary Boundary Treaty (Paudyal, July-December 2013). The Treaty of Perpetual Peace and Friendship between Great Britain and Nepal was signed on December 21, 1923 (Nepal Embassy UK, undated and Bhusal, March 2020), establishing diplomatic relations with Nepal and India. Thus, Britain became the first country in the world that established its Embassy in Kathmandu. While returning back to *Naya Muluk*, the Treaty was signed between Nepal's Prime Minister Jung Bahadur Rana and British Lieutenant General George Ramsay (Mulmi, October 1, 2017). A map was also updated which clearly showed that Nepal's western border was mentioned up to Limpiyadhura. On January 7, 1975, the British East India Company published another map of Nepal on the course to demarcate the boundary of Dang district; Limpiyadhura was mentioned as Nepal's western border.

Nepo-India demarcates the borders or boundary lines based on the Articles 3 and 5 of the Sugauli Treaty. The Article 3 said, "(3.1) The whole of the lowlands between the

20

Rivers Kali and Rapti; (3.2) The whole of the low lands (with the exception of Bootwul Khass) lying between the Rapti and the Gunduck; (3.3) The whole of the lowlands between the Gunduck and Coosah, in which the authority of the British Government has been introduced, or is in actual course of introduction; (3.4) All the lowlands between the Rivers Mitchee and the Teestah; and (3.5) All the territories within the hills eastward of the River Mitchee including the fort and lands of Nagree and the Pass of Nagarcote leading from Morung into the hills, together with the territory lying between that pass and nagerr. The aforesaid territory shall be evacuated by the Gorkha troops soon from signed date."

The west boundary as Kali River was delineated by Article 5 of the Treaty of Sugauli which says, "The Rajas of Nepal renounces for himself, his heirs, and successors, all claim to or connection with the countries lying to the west of the River Kali and engages never to have any concern with those countries or the inhabitants thereof" Nepal development, undated). The Kali River marked the western border of Nepal, but there is no clear agreement on what is the accurate location of the Kali River, and whether the disputed land consisting of Kalapani-Limpiyadhura-Lipulek is part of present day Nepal or India. Some scholars suggest that Kali River shifted over time or made artificial Kali River with the vested interest of India.

No map was attached with the Sugauli Treaty, as the Treaty was drafted by the East-India Company without the consent of Nepal. Kalapani, Lipulek Pass, Nabi, Gunji, Kuti and Limpiyadhura are parts of the Nepali territory which as supported by many facts, evidence and testimonies. The historic boundary maps of 1819, 1827, 1850, 1856, 1879 and 1905, among others, depicted that Kali River is western border of Nepal. The Nepal boundary is extended from which the Kali River originating from Limpiyadhura (Shrestha, June 27, 2015) as agreed upon in the Sugauli Treaty. British Survey of India has clearly portrayed the Kali River by the historic maps of 1827 and 1856. In India's 1856 map, the origin of Mahakali is shown at Limpiyadhura (Budhathoki, November 11, 2019). On January 2, 1816, Arrowsmith published a map from London which clearly identified the River emanating from Limpiyadhura (Manandhar & Koirala, June 2001).

A map of the Old Atlas of China (1903), in Chinese Characters, published during Qing Dynasty, depicted Limpiyadhura as the source of the Kali River, the north-eastern part of the river (Shrestha, June 22, 2015). As scholar S D Muni said, "The maps issued by the British between 1816 and 1860 generally favour the Nepali position. But, the maps issued afterwards endorse India's position. It is possible that the British administration changed this position through proper surveys or subsequently decided to manipulate this position to serve its larger strategic and commercial interests in using the Lipulek Pass for access to Tibet. Independent India was given access to Kalapani and Lipulek by the British" (May 22, 2020). However, Muni failed to provide viable arguments with facts and evidence without the dates of maps issued by India. Immediately after the inauguration of link-road via Lipulek Pass, Muni mentioned that the inaccessible Kalapani area belonged to Nepal and India could take those lands in lease for years through dialogue. It is sad to say that, later, Muni changed his stands along with the line of statements of Government of India.

It is to be remarkable that neither the returning of lowlands (December 11, 1816) and *Naya Muluk* (November 1, 1860), nor Sino-Nepal Treaty of Peace and Friendship (Sino-Nepalese Border Treaty) of October 5, 1961, had singed any Treaties regarding the western border (Kali River) of Nepal. The Nepo-India interpretation of origin of Kali River is different.

Nepo-China Boundary Treaty signed by King Mahendra in Beijing on October 5, 1961 made a reference to the Limpiyadhura and the Kali River. The Article 1 stated, "The Chinese - Nepalese boundary line starts from the point where the watershed between the Kali River and the Tinkar River meets the watershed between the tributaries of the Mapchu (Karnali) River on the one hand and the Tinkar River on the other hand... passing through the Niumachisa (Limpiyadhura)..."
(fall.fsulawrc.com/collection/LimitsinSeas/IBS050.pdf).

The Government of India has constructed a temple along, with an artificial lake and artificial Kali River, in front of the temple at the Kalapani. The frozen water outlets through a small tap and joins with the Lipu River. Thus, India claims this is an origination of Kali River and has developed several military (border security) posts in and around Kalapani, Limpiyadhura and Lipulek areas. However, Nepal claims that the river which flows from Limpiyadhura is considered the origin of Kali River (Tuladhar et al, September/October 1999). Clarifying the origin of Kali River, Avantika Regmi writes, "After Nepal's defeat at Almora on June 1, 1815, Lord Hastings, Governor-General of British India, in a secret letter wrote, 'The Eastern boundary of Kali (Kumaon) will be from the snow-capped mountains to the plains almost directly to the South'". She further asks, "Did he think of Kalapani waterfall or Lipu River while writing this?" (November 29, 2019). Based on the historical maps preserved in the British Museum Library and the Library of Congress in the United States, Buddhi Narayan Shrestha says, "The Head of Mahakali is Limpiyadhura" (Naya Patrika, May 13, 2020).

While the Anglo-Nepalese War (November 1, 1814-March 4, 1816) had been going on, the Governor General of India sent a secret letter to the Secret Committee of the East India Company, London on June 1, 1815 stating the Kali River shall be the eastern boundary of East India with Nepal (Bhusal, March 2020). The secret letter stated, "The Kali forms a well-defined boundary from the snowy mountains to the plains, and though narrow, it is deep and rapid. The snowy range ... touches the eastern confines of Kumaon. Hence this is the shortest, and consequently the most defensible line of frontier" (Cox, 1824) (see, Figure – 1 & 2).

Figure 1 & 2: Map of Kali (Kalee) River, Limpiyadhura, Lipulek, Kuti, Nabi, Gunj, and Kalapani

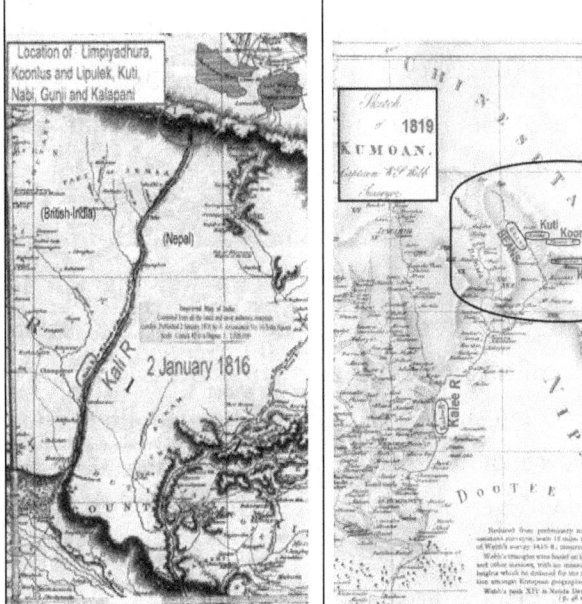

Figure 1: Kali river as the international borderline between British-India and Nepal (www.davidrumsey.com)	**Figure 2:** The uppermost reach of Kali river as the western borderline between British-India and Nepal (pahar.in/indian-subcontinent-pre-1899)

Note: The map was published by the East India Company when British India and Nepal signed the Sugauli Treaty on December 2, 1815. Figure 2 showed the pictorial clarification of the secret letter written by Lord Moira in 1815 (Cox, 1824).

Source: Evolution of cartographic aggression by India: A study of Limpiyadhura to Lipulek, March 2020

Article 5 of the Sugauli Treaty clearly states that the western border of Nepal is the Kali River, which is now called Mahakali in Nepal and Sarada in India. Figure 1 demarcates the headstream of Kali River. The maps of 1819, 1827, 1834, 1835, 1837 1846, 1848, 1850, and 1856 had demarcated the Kali River which originates from Limpiyadhura Bhusal, March 2020).

Bhairab Risal (a 93 year old senior journalist of Nepal and the then Government Officer) who led the Population Census in 1961 stated that he had recorded details of each household of all settlements including the villages of Kuti Nabi, and Gunji situated on the east of Kali River (June 11, 2015). Old records of land ownership rights in Kuti, Nabi, and Gunji villages are available in the Land Administration Office, Doti district, which proves the Limpiyadhura belongs to Nepal (Bhusal, March 2020).

In the part of "The Kingdom of Nepal" in *A Geographical, Statistical, and Historical Description of Hindostan, and the Adjacent Countries* (1971), written by Walter Hamilton, stated the Kali River is the western section of the Gogra River (Shah, November 13, 2019). There were several maps published by the Survey of British India in 1816, 1819, 1827, 1830, 1834, 1835, 1837, 1841, 1846, and 1856, among others, clearly stating the origin of Kali River west of Gogra River (Mulyankan, September/October 1999). Nepali nationals claim even those. On a pilgrimage to Mount Kailash and Mansarovar Lake they are not permitted to enter the Kalapani area and the Lipulek Pass, their sovereign territory. On the other, issues of the Lipulek-Kalapani-Limpiyadhura area have long been neglected and largely ignored by the Nepali authorities fearing India's 4Ps of power, politics, property, and privilege. The dispute in the Kalapani area could not be solved even if India became independent from the colony of British and if India introduced Nehruvian socialism.

After Nepal proclaimed a democratic country freed from the anarchical rule of Ranas for 104 years, on November 16, 1951, Matrika Prasad Koirala became Prime Minister of Nepal, ousting Mohan Shumsher JB Rana. He visited New Delhi on January 6, 1952. Koirala requested PM Nehru to help send the Indian Army to reorganize, train, and empower as well as ease planning for the Nepal Army (Pathak, September 15, 2014). And Nehru accepted the oral proposal (December 2010).

Even though, Nehru had been ambiguous about whether to send troops to assist Nepal. He asked, "sending India troops to Nepal had been the wish or demand of Government of Nepal or instructed by his own Ambassador Singh, residing in Kathmandu". That shows how very much powerful the Indian ambassador in Kathmandu was. He had a fear of how international communities would react to the move. Given letters (in Boxes – III & IV) of communication to the Indian Ambassadors to Nepal, one shall understand how much

Nehru was confused to send troops to Nepal as he was deeply bonded by democratic-socialism.

Indian PM Nehru became ready to send troops at the request of the Government of Nepal. Both Nepo-Indian Prime Ministers agreed to provide security for Indian Embassy, Airport, and other strategically important places, which was headed by Major General. Besides, the Indian Ambassador started attending all Ministry of Council meetings and interventing in the decisions initiated thereafter. Cowan writes, "The Indian ambassador from 1949 to 1952, C. P. N. Singh, played a key part in the 1950 revolution, and his meddling in the affairs of the Nepali Congress Party and the shaping of Nepali Government policy was notorious" (December 14, 2015). However, King Tribhuvan himself had been very active in the course of seeking Indian guidance to protect the Panchayat autocratic rules.

Box - III

January 30, 1952

Letter of the Indian Prime Minister Jawaharlal Nehru to the India Ambassador in Nepal Chandreshwar Prasad Narain Singh

New Delhi, India

My Dear Chandreshwar;

The whole incident about our sending our troops to Kathmandu has disturbed me. I wrote a letter to you this afternoon, before my last talk with you on the telephone, I enclose this letter. Since then of course we have come to the decision not to send any troop.

Late this evening the Nepalese Ambassador here, General Bijaya, saw K.P.S. Menon and said that there was no necessity for sending our troops.

All this is very mysterious that it shows how we may make grave mistakes if we are not careful every step. The Nepalese Government has not got great experiences and is apt to think about their own particular situation forgetting other aspects. I shall have to be very careful in future about any message that I get from them.

Yours sincerely

Jawaharlal Nehru

Source: Nepal-India Boundary: River Kali as International Boundary, June 2001.

It is to be noted that both official letters were written on the same day. K.P.S. (Kumara Padma Sivasankara) Menon had been a Secretary of the Ministry of Foreign Affairs, New Delhi and Bijaya Shumsher Jung Bahadur Rana had been working as a Nepalese Ambassador to India, New Delhi.

On February 27, 1952 (101 days after Nepal's request), the Indian Army Mission (IAM) finally landed in Kathmandu for a year. The IAM changed its name to Indian Military Training and Adventure Group (IMTAG) later. Beyond providing training to Nepal Army, the IMTAG moved towards the Northern Himalayas (strategic important locations on the course to watch the activities of Tibet, China) and established military posts across the frontier.

On November 7, 1950 (before the Indian Army arrived in Nepal), the Iron Man of India (Deputy PM and Home Minister Sardar Vallabhbhai Patel) wrote a letter to PM Nehru stating how India was being made insecure by China. He writes, "The political and administrative steps which we should take to strengthen our northern and north-eastern frontier. This would include the whole border, i.e., Nepal, Bhutan, Sikkim, Darjeeling, and tribal territory of Assam" (www.friendsoftibet.org/sardarpatel.html).

Box - IV

New Delhi, January 30, 1952

My Dear Ambassador;

Kathmandu, Nepal

Since the receipt your message yesterday morning, conveying the desire of the Government of Nepal for Indian troops to be sent Kathmandu, we have given a great deal of thought to this matter. This message troubled us, because we do not like at all the prospects of our troops going to Kathmandu, especially at the present juncture. At the same time, if there was real need for them and there was some danger of trouble in Kathmandu, then we could not take the risk of refuging the Nepal Government's request. After much thought and after telephonic communication with you, we declared to send our troops as intimated to you.

 Yours sincerely

Jawaharlal Nehru

Source: Nepal-India Boundary: River Kali as
        International Boundary, June 2001.

For each check-post, 20 to 40 Indian army officials equipped with arms and ammunition along with communication equipment, were deployed (Shrestha, January 1, 2003). A few Nepali army and civilian officials were also associated with them. India substantially intensified its monitoring of a number of military groups in 18 check-posts, increasingly fearing the growing Chinese threat. In March 1959, the tensions between Indian-China increased in the wake of the revolt in Tibet by Dalai Lama, who later flew to India (Whelpton, June 2016) on March 30, 1959, along with his retinue with the help of the CIA's special efforts (Richardson, 1984). Sometime later, Lama set up a Government in Tibet in exile in Dharmashala, India (Jackson, February 29, 2009). Since that time, the relationship between India and China has remained anonymous and competitive, which always hits Nepal hard.

Buddhi Narayan Shrestha, in his book *Border Management of Nepal* (January 1, 2003), stated that the Indian Military started being sent back to India by the Government of Nepal on April 20, 1969. Dissatisfied with the decision, India threatened Nepal to close the border but was finally compelled to withdraw all check-posts by August 1970. Thus, the Indian Army Mission finally returned in more than 18 years. It stayed an additional 17 years than initially agreed for one year only. Neither Nepal initiated any objection to having the Indian troops were established in Kalapani (Darchula) in 1960, nor did India take permission from the Government of Nepal (Naya Patrika, May 20, 2020).

The issue of Kalapani attracted all sections of Nepalese people, comprising general people, students, teachers, bureaucrats or other professionals, civil society or human rights activists, and political leaders. On June 26, 1996, a 39-membei Public-level Border Encroachment Prevention Committee was formed to study the complete facts and truths of the Kalapani area under the leadership of veteran human rights activist Padma Ratna Tuladhar. High-profile stalwarts of all professions were included on the Committee. The Committee collected huge documents and testimonies including taxes villagers of lands of Tinkar, Kunji, Bundi, Chhangru, and Nabi (byas gorkka areas) paid at the Land Revenue Office, Darchula till December 1940 (Mulyankan, September/October 1999).

It is to be noted that Residents of the Nabi, Gunji, and Kuti villages of the Kalapani area used to pay *Bali* (land revenue) to the concerned district authority of Darchula, Government of Nepal until 1978 (Sharma, May 30, 2020) (Annex III). Bhuwan Sharma writes, "The government has safely kept the receipts of land taxes paid by Ratan Budha (Tinkar), Panchhyaura Budha (Budi), Mohan Singh Budha (Gabryang), Hari Singh Budha (Gunji), and Hari Krishna Budha (Nabi)" (Sharma, May 30, 2020). And they obtained Nepali citizenship certificates too.

Almost all Chief District Officers (including Dr. Dwarika Nath Dhungel and Mohan Acharya) of the Darchula district from the Panchayat regimes to the Democratic Government 1990, sent reports of the activities of semi-military posts situated in the Kalapani area to the concerned authorities in Kathmandu; neither the high-level officials disclosed the crisis of Kalapani territory to the public Nordic they listen to the reports of the CDOs. Apart from that, they were busy with sycophancy with India and Indian authorities for the sake of saving their state-power and earning money from India continuously as a milking cow.

Nepo-India boundary is 1,880 km long, of which 1,240 km have land boundaries erecting boundary pillars and 640 km. have river and rivulet (water boundary) boundary lines. It has counted 60 rivers and rivulets and boundary lines were about 200 km long constituting the Mahakali River, western boundary, and about 80 km Mechi River, eastern boundary. The Gandak River is 20 km long, which makes the boundary to Susta. There are another 57 rivers and rivulets with lengths of 340 km (Baral, December 2019). The boundary lines between Nepal-India were surveyed and demarcated from 1816 to 1860, 1882, 1885, 1906, 1930 to 1931, and 1940 to 1941, dividing into nine different segments erecting masonry boundary pillars (Baral, December 2019).

None of Nepali population knows the understanding reached between King Mahendra (1955-1972) and India's first PM, Jawaharlal Nehru, but the Limpiyadhura triangle remained in limbo. The monocracy Panchayat era (1960-1990) had been a time of closed administrators in which the Government officials of the Darchula district directly reported to the Narayanhiti Royal Palace, both King Mahendra and his son King Birendra.

The then Finance Minister Rishikesh Shah (interacting with Mahendra shortly after the monarch's coup on December 15, 1960) stated that King Mahendra received information about the encroachment in the Kalapani areas when it happened. Shah remembered that, when the matter of Kalapani was reported to King Mahendra. Mahendra replied, "India is quite angry with me, let's not anger them further right now. Let them stay in Kalapani for now" (Cowan, December 14, 2015).

However, both Kings remained quiet forever. Even after the restoration of democracy, the democratic leaders turned deaf ears having the establishment of Indian military posts in the Kalapani areas. They were kept quiet till the Mahakali Treaty (1995-1996)[ii] was ratified which resulted in split of the CPN (Marxist-Leninist) from its mother party CPN (UML) stating "Mahakali Treaty was treasonous" (Shrestha, June 16, 2020). The issue of Kalapani was intensified by the splinter group. Mahakali has been a hot debate since then. The Mahakali Treaty has made Nepalese hearts cry. Mahakali is common, water is shared 'half-and-half', but this is in vain in practice. The river has dried up while India has taken whole water from the canal alone (Kafle & Baral,

June 16, 2020) in the winter season and flooded Nepal side in summer.

On May 11, 2020, Nepal's Foreign Minister Pradip Gyawali called the India Ambassador Vinay Kwatra to Kathmandu for a meeting and handed over a diplomatic note against the road construction, conveying the Government of Nepal's position on boundary lines and issues and a similar note was submitted to the Ministry of External Affairs, New Delhi (The Wire Staff, May 11, 2020, & MOFA Nepal, May 11, 2020). But, such notes have not formally been acknowledged. Nepal's PM K. P. Oli had a high expectation of having a virtual exchanging and sharing of the catastrophe with the Indian Counter Part Modi which was scheduled for May 19, but Modi canceled the meeting unilaterally (Pandey, Sapkota and Dahal, May 26, 2020). On August 15, 2020, PM Oli and his Indian counterpart Modi held a 15 minute telephone conversation while Oli extended wishes to Modi on the auspicious Independence Day of India (Republica, August 15, 2020), but this was in vain on talk of Kapapani border disputes. There has been a communication gap on the issue of Kalapani areas until the mid of 2022.

As a result, on May 20, 2020, Nepal released its new politico-administrative map, the first since the signing of the Treaty of Sugauli in 1816, including territories of Kalapani areas that have long been claimed by both Nepal and India (Giri, May 21, 2020). The Ministry of Land

Management has collected and analyzed as many as 132 maps for facts and shreds of evidence before replacing the existing map with the new one. Even in the maps prepared by India, Kalapani, Lipulek, and Limpiyadhura regions have been placed on the Nepali side (Sharma, May 30, 2020).

An all-party meeting held at the Prime Minister's residence on May 26, 2020, forged a consensus among the Parliamentary parties (The Rising Nepal, May 26, 2020) to amend the Constitution on the course to update an official cartographic map of the country along with the emblem of Nepal.

On June 18, 2020, President Bidhya Devi Bhandari signed the Constitution Amendment Bill for changing the existing map of Nepal, including Lipulek, Kalapani, and Limpiyadhura. The new amendment Bill was unanimously endorsed by the Upper and Lower Houses of the Federal Parliament of Nepal (Republica, June 19, 2020) stating Lipulek, Limpiyadhura, and Kalapani as Nepal's integral territory (Ghimire, June 18, 2020). None of the lawmakers voted against it in both National Assembly and Lower House.

History reveals that the peaceful coexistence and harmonious and friendly relations between two nations sometimes turned into disagreement while the concerned bureaucrats and security personnel misinformed their bosses (Head of the State and top-most political leaders).

And decisions were taken accordingly. Such a trend is repeated in India (Pathak, September 14, 2015).

The Eminent Persons Group (EPG) on Nepo-India relations was established in January 2016 to review and regulate the Nepo-India border; to recommend revision or replacement of the 1950 Peace Treaty; to issue smart cards for the people of both nations crossing either side of the border, and to jointly work for combating terrorism and controlling smuggling of fake-currency, human trafficking, and other illegal activities (Subedi, Undated).

On June 30, 2018, the EPG had prepared a single report by consensus (Giri, July 1, 2018). Indian PM Modi is reluctant to receive the report despite huge pressure from his colleagues. There has been an allegation that, before the submission of the EPG Report to PM Modi, a core part of it was delivered to China by Dr. Rajan Bhattarai (https://gundrukkhabar.com/backup/18058/), the then Foreign Advisor of PM of Nepal. Therefore, the EPG Report has created controversy.

On January 1, 2018, or 15 days prior to K P Sharma Oli became second times PM of Nepal, Indian External Affairs Minister Smt. Sushma Swaraj arrived in Kathmandu. The most obvious objective of the agenda was to further strengthen the relationship between the two adjoining countries (Government of India, January 29, 2018), but a hidden agenda-less (purpose-less) visit was to convey the best wishes and warm message of Indian PM Narendra Modi to Oli as a forthcoming powerful (almost two-thirds majority at the House holding) Communist PM of Nepal and invite him to visit in India as soon as possible.

On January 1, 2018, there had been a one-to-one meeting (between Oli and Swaraj) for more than an hour before the official delegation meeting held between the top CPN (UML) leaders and Indian officials at Soaltee Hotel. There had been a general trend to congratulate and invite to visit India to newly appointed PM immediately after the oath of administration in Nepal. It was the first time in the history that the Indian Ministry of External Affairs with their senior official team visited Nepal just to congratulate the forthcoming PM of Nepal.

There were two obvious reasons. First, the first ever formation of a powerful communist government meant to lean toward India, creating distance to China. On the other hand, from the time Oli became the President of the Youth Federation (sister organization of the CPN-UML), Oli in many cases worked in favor of India to fulfill its aspirations even going against the wishes and sentiment to Nepali people, i.e., Mahakali Treaty. That meant congratulations to Oli from the bottom of India's heart and to send a good message to all including China that India was on Oli's side.

When PM Oli broke the gentlemen's agreement held between Prachanda and himself to run the government for two and a half years by each, Oli felt in the minority in the party and parliament. After Oli tried hard to ratify the MCC without any amendment from the parliament, he went further into weakness within the CPN.

To stay being strong as Prime Minister in Nepal, Oli appointed all 52 courtiers as the members of the Constitutional Bodies proclaiming Ordinances on the course to boycott the constitutional provision of parliamentary hearings. The Constitution of Nepal 2015 says,

> "Provisions relating to parliamentary hearings: (1) Parliamentary hearings shall be conducted as to appointments to the offices of the Chief Justice and Judges of the Supreme Court, members of the Judicial Council, chiefs and members of Constitutional Bodies, who are appointed on the recommendation of the Constitutional Council under this Constitution, and to the offices of ambassadors, as provided for in the Federal law. (2) For the purposes of clause (1), there shall be formed a fifteen member joint committee consisting of members of both Houses of the Federal Parliament, in accordance with the Federal law" (Article 292).

In early December 2020, a writ has been filed in the Supreme Court against the Constitutional Council Ordinance brought by the Oli-led Government. Advocates Om Prakash Aryal, Dinesh Tripathi, and Punya Prasad Khatiwada have filed a writ petition against the President's Office, the Prime Minister, the Council of Ministers, and the Constitutional Council.

Surprisingly, the Supreme Court has not yet decided till the end of June 2022 on the writ petition against the Constitutional Council Ordinance. The reluctance is that Oli recruited almost all the judges in the court as his courtiers. Oli is not influencing the court alone; India is also behind him. India has a strong and hidden presence in all the executive, judiciary, and legislative departments in Nepal.

Despite the unification of the CPN (UML) and the CPN (Maoist Center) into the CPN in May 2018, the Supreme Court ordered the restoration of the UML and the Maoist Center before the merger position in March 2021. PM Oli and India were very keen to strengthen the UML by formally splitting the Maoist Center from the mother CPN party. For this specific purpose, both Oli and India, who were highly pressured and influenced the Supreme Court by providing huge sums of bribes for such a decision, have been widely discussed till the date.

Even though Oli dissolved the House twice with the lure of staying in power and the Supreme Court reinstated it both times, Nepali Congress President Sher Bahadur Deuba was appointed as the new Prime Minister of Nepal on July 13, 2021, after the Supreme Court overturned both of Oli's dissolutions. Notwithstanding that, only the Indian Ambassador to Nepal, Vinay Mohan Kwatra, visited the House of the Deuba and congratulated him. Here the question arises, why did India feel difficulty congratulating the new PM Deuba unlike Oli and other past PMs? How long will these selfish politics of India last? Anti-India sentiment is developing in Nepal due to the policy of treating one as near and the other as far. As a result, Nepalis tend to tilt towards China.

3. Protests and Arguments of Nepal

Nepal said that India's road connectivity to China is an encroachment on its national integrity, independence, security, and sovereignty. Since the announcement of the inauguration of a link road to Mansarovar on May 9, 2020, by India, sporadic protests took place in the capital, Kathmandu, and other major cities across the country. The street protests intensified along with the effigies of the Indian PM Modi. Shouting slogans against the Government of India, many agitated youths affiliated with parties came on the streets with Modi's effigies and slapped the faces of effigies with sandals, and finally burned them despite violating the lockdown restrictions. Many of such agitated youths were arrested by police and kept in detention centers for a while. The Federal Parliament of Nepal directed the Government of Nepal to issue a new Nepal map, including Kalapani areas as its territory. Nepo-India shares an open and porous border that is distinctive in South Asia.

On May 10, 2020, the Ministry of Foreign Affairs released a press statement that said, "The Government of Nepal learned with regret about the 'inauguration' yesterday by India of 'Link Road' connecting to Lipulek (Nepal), which passes through Nepali territory. This unilateral act runs against the understanding reached between the two countries, including at the level of Prime Ministers, that a solution to boundary issues would be sought through negotiation" (Giri, May 10, 2020).

On May 10, 2020, All Nepal National Free Students Union (ANNFSU) members, the student wing of the ruling Nepal Communist Party, were arrested in the course of protesting against India's inauguration of a link road to Mansarovar via Kalapani Lipulek areas, claiming the areas belong to Nepali territory (Khabarhub.com, May 9, 2020). On May 11, 2020, some furious Nepali protestors burned effigies of both PM Modi and PM Oli in Babarmahal, Kathmandu, crossing the restriction zones (Desh Sanchar, May 11, 2020) of the CORONA-19 lockdown. Similarly, conscious people of Baitadi district, far west of Nepal (Ujyalo online, June 30, 2019), and Pokhara, western Nepal, also burned effigies of PM Modi (Online Khabar, May 10, 2020).

On May 12, 2020, human rights activists, including Krishna Pahadi, were arrested and detained by police while they were staging an anti-India protest against the link road announcement outside the Indian Embassy in Kathmandu. The link road passes through Gunj village of the Nepali territory (Online Khabar, May 12, 2020). On May 11, 2020, Aljazeera telecasted, "Nepal has protested against India's inauguration of a Himalayan link road built in a disputed territory which falls at a strategic three-way junction".

Nepal lost Sikkim, including Darjeeling, the territories of Kumaon, Garhwal, Dehra Dun, and most of the lowlands of the Tarai. The Mechi River became the new eastern border and the Mahakali River the western boundary of Nepal (Article 5 of the Sugauli Treat). As a result, more than one-third controlled territories of Nepal had been given to British India. The Treaty established a British representative in Kathmandu (Thakur and Sahani, July 2018). Article 9 of the Sugauli Treaty said, "This treaty shall be ratified by the King of Nepal within 15 days from this date, and the ratification shall be delivered to Lt. Col. Bradshaw, who engages to obtain and deliver to the King the ratification of the Governor-General within 20 days, or sooner, if practicable. There shall be perpetual peace and friendship between the East India Company and Nepal".

But, Nepal failed to ratify the Treaty by King Girvan Yuddha Bikram Shah during said period. British-India had been well aware that Nepali did not agree with the unilaterally drafted Treaty; the British had felt they had done some kind of injustice to the Gorkha Army (Shrestha, November 2008). To console the Gorkha army, they provided two Lakhs of Nepalese Currencies annually as compensation (Indian-Board, November 8, 1816) for the loss of *Jagirs* (employments) in the Tarai. The Tarai lands made it difficult for the British to govern and some of them between Rapti and Koshi, including Chitwan and Makwanpur (forest and grass jungles), were returned to

46

Nepal Government (Oldfield, 1880) on December 11, 1816, as a gratuitous boon and the annual payments NRs 200,000 abolished accordingly (Mulyankan, September/October 1999).

Author Bishnu Pathak in his *Nepal-India Relations: Open Secret Diplomacy stated that* The British East India Company prepared the manuscript of the Treaty unilaterally imposed and signed by Lieutenant Colonel Paris Bradshaw on December 2, 1815, Saturday without the consent of the Government of Nepal. However, the signed document was sent to Nepal with a 15-day ultimatum for the signature. Nepal Government did not feel comfortable with the terms and conditions mentioned in the Treaty. As a result, Nepal did not sign it within the said period. The Company then spread a rumor, stating that they would be launching an attack on Kathmandu displaying the strength of the military forces (May 31, 2009).

As Nepal realized that attack on the capital had been on the door, the Government had been forced to agree with the manuscript of the Treaty for the signature. Nepal Government decided that none of the King and other high-ranking officials should sign it. Therefore, Nepal was sent to sign by Raj Guru Gajraj Mishra, aided by Chandra Sekhar Upadhaya. On March 4, 1816, Monday, Mishra signed the Treaty named Sugowlee (Sugauli) at the British East India Company camp. Instead of 15 days ultimatum, the Sugauli Treaty was signed after 94 days, and the Treaty came into effect on the same day. In 1815, the British East India Company Major General Sir David Ochterlony evicted the Nepalese with brutality from Garhwal and Kumaon west of the Kali River, finally ending 12 years of Nepalese occupation, and he was compelled to offer the peace to Nepal in the name of Sugauli Treaty (Oakley, 1905).

In an interaction at a defense think-tank, Indian Army Chief General MM Naravane mentioned Beijing as the activating force for Kathmandu's objection and said, "The area east of Kali River belongs to them. The road that we built is on the west of the river. There was no dispute. I don't know what they are agitating about. There has never been any problem in the past. There is reason to believe that they might have raised the issues at the behest of someone else, and that is very much a possibility" (The Economic Times, May 15, 2020). That controversial remark was protested by all quarters, including individuals and institutions (Republica, May 16, 2020). The territorial disputes have been made a difficult resolution and transformation by Dialogue means on the Lipulek Pass matter. There is no need to drag China on the Nepo-India disputed issues. And Nepal is a sovereign state and firmly believes in the principle of peaceful coexistence and non-alignment.

The controversy of territorial disputes created a substantial political and Government hullaballoo, both inland and in neighboring India. While the Prime Minister of Nepal Oli faced mounting criticism from both the ruling party and beyond (South Asia, June 29, 2020), he commented, "Plots are being hatched to topple me for releasing the country's new map and getting it adopted through Parliament. Given the ongoing intellectual discussions, media reports from New Delhi, [Indian] embassy's activities, and meetings at different hotels in Kathmandu, it is not very difficult to understand how people are actively trying to unseat me" (Pradhan, June 29, 2020). PM Oli believed that, after the adoption of a new politico-administrative map in Nepal, in-party leaders with support from India were plotting to topple him from the Government. Consequently, he had become a young wounded tiger.

Speaking at an event having poet Bhanubhakta's birth anniversary, PM Oli said, "We did not give Sita, who was born in Janakpur, to an Indian Prince but Sita was married to Ram of Ayodhya, not of India. There is a huge controversy in 'their' Ayodhya while our Ayodhya that lies in the Thori village has no issues as such" (The Himalayan Times, July 14, 2020) in central Tarai of Nepal. This is no less than a tricky trump card of PM Oli. He spoke to provoke India rather than stating that Ram was born in Ayodhya, Nepal. Nepal has a great anti-India people's sentiment. And, PM Oli continues to his State power with the support of these masses. His card also failed as the Government of India did not formally respond and neglected his alleged speech.

Figure 4: Political map of Nepal with Kalapani, Lepulekh, and Limpiyadhura

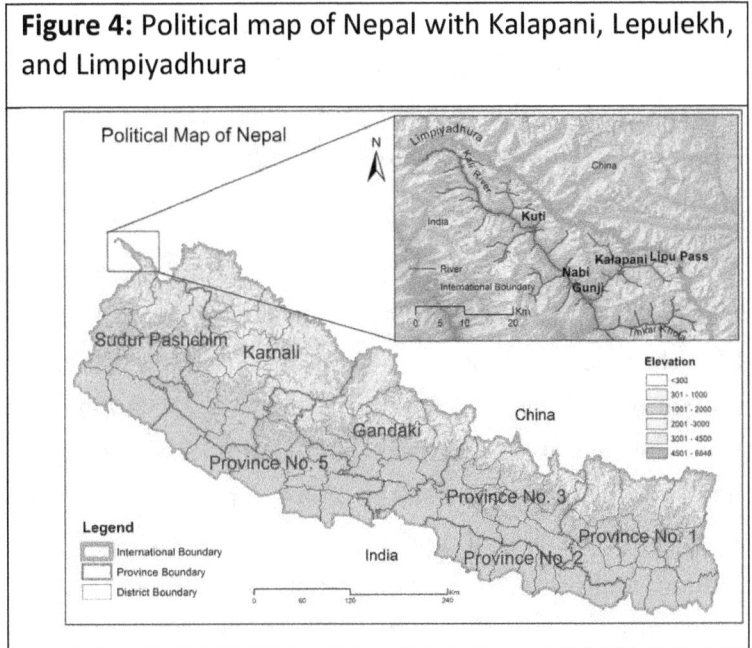

Source: Government of Nepal, 2020

Political scientist Krishna Pokhrel says, "We have always been reactive, not proactive, on the border issue with India. Only if we can create a conducive situation for talks being proactive; sooner or later Kalapani, Limpiyadhura, and Lipulek will get justice" (May 13, 2020). Sponsored Indian journalists weave a web of fictitious allegations and conspiracies and have transmitted, having the illicit relationship between the PM Oli and the Chinese Ambassador in Kathmandu. Nepal Government Spokesman Yubaraj Khatiwada announced, "Some Indian media outlets made baseless and shameful allegations against PM Oli and Kathmandu will take legal and political action against the Indian media" (EurAsian Times, July 11, 2020). That resulted in banning some private Indian Television news channels in Nepal.

In response to a letter to the local administration of Darchula (India) on July 14, 2020, Nepal has asked the Dharchula local administration of India not to restrict the movement of Nepalis to enter into Gunj, Kalapani, and Limpiyadhura areas. The letter states that Nepalese people have every right to enter the aforementioned territories and no hindrances should be put in their movement by Indian authorities as these areas fall within Nepal's boundaries as per the Sugauli Treaty, east of Kali River (Republica, July 29, 2020, & Das, July 30, 2020).

Article 1 of the Peace and Friendship Treaty 1950 says, "…The two Governments agree mutually to acknowledge and respect the complete sovereignty, territorial integrity, and independence of each other". However, there had been fictitious information developed regarding the entry (original) source of the Kali River. India has been gradual shifting borderlines from 1 to 6 (Figure 5) cartographic aggression in the north-west border of Nepal (Bhusal, March 2020). India has already kept holding Lipulek pass solely within its territory (The Survey of India, 1960 and Surveyor General of India, 1961). Bhusal writes, "The Nepal-China border agreement treaty of 1961 has marked

No-1 pillar at the Tinker and Karnali watersheds. This had motivated India to push cartographically Nepal's border to a few kilometers south-east of Lipulek, to the meeting point of watersheds of Karnali, Tinker, and Lipu" (March 2020).

Figure 5: Map showing cartographic falsifications (Borderlines No 1 to No 6) and areas

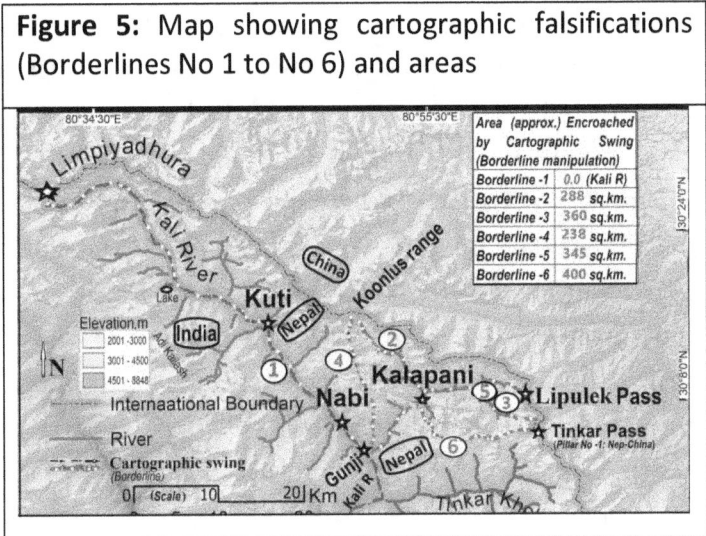

Source: Evolution of cartographic aggression by India: A study of Limpiyadhura to Lipulek, March 2020

It would be unjust to insult India alone. There is a well-known fact that, after the restoration of democracy in 1990, Nepali leaders were vying for India's blessings to attain power in the Party and Government of Nepal. For that specific purpose, there is a long list of leaders who visited India in the name of treatment and secretly met establishment forces and other leaders to attain more powerful-successful advantages in Nepal. Nepali leaders have not only received financial support for their livelihood from India, but India has been providing moral, political, sanctuary, and other protection to them.

Ambitious Nepalese leaders have encouraged and invited India to intervene up to this level of territorial disputes. India started to construct the road from Kalapani to Lipulek Pass along with the 12-point understanding signed between the seven parliament parties and the CPN (Maoist) in New Delhi on November 21, 2005. Since then, 11 Prime Ministers including monarc[iii] have already been appointed in Nepal, but none of them raised questions having the territories of Kalapani, Susta areas, and many other border disputed areas. Buddhi Narayan Shrestha says, "As Nepal did not resist, India built a road at Lipulek" (May 20, 2020).

There is ample history of India's assistance being used by Nepal's many leaders. Many leaders are not doing politics to provide service to the people, but for their ultimate goal, for the choice of profession is for their own family/courtier livelihood. The priority of each adult is to become a Doctor or Engineer. And, second, to become a Government employee (civil servant). The third is to get a job in a corporate body, including a bank. The fourth is a teacher, and the fifth is business. Many people who failed to achieve the above-mentioned opportunities or businesses, finally enroll as a political cadre. The above priorities or classifications are observed and analyzed based on the comments of general Nepalese people. It happened because of highly proliferated cronyism in Nepal.

Even educated have been able to stay in power through sycophancy, but they have failed to serve the people too. For instance, the outgoing Finance Minister Dr. Yuba Raj Khatiwada. The level of Khatiwada could not go above those of cadres. He has a sharp intention to please the leader(s) and grasp the opportunities time and again following nepotism, favoritism, and sycophancy as well as brokering needed assistance to his commander(s). Against Khatiwada's incompetence, prejudiced eyes, and discrimination, a case has been registered in the Supreme Court in 2019. The preliminary hearing of the Court puts the case on priority.

On September 22, 2015, Prachanda, in Tudikhel's speech, publicly expressed his unhappiness with PM Modi's special envoy Subrahmanyam Jaishankar and how he humiliated and disrespected him (Pathak, 2015). The same Jaishankar is now working as a Minister for External Affairs. His appointment as Minister is intended to implement the US Millennium Challenge Corporation in Nepal as per their vested interest.

Unlike China's apology and compensation to Nepal in July 1960, India neither expressed an apology nor sought compensation to the Koshi dam victims (Pathak,

September 12, 2008), inundation in Tarai-Madhes, and border encroachment.

How gentle, honest, and docile Nepalese people are. Nepalese people seek prosperous and developed Nepal from such self- or broker-centered and, many occasions, failed leaders. Nepal never achieved 'politics is the service to the people' and politics has been a 'profession' in a multi-party democracy. In Republican Nepal, politics has become the Pewa (private property) of the influential leader of the Party.

The absolute truth is that such a principal leader tries to compel other leaders of the party to accept his/her unilateral decision. Such a one-man decision escalated the conflict within its party and split in the past. The dream of socialism, which has been guaranteed by the Nepalese Constitution 2015, is to accept the collective decisions of the concerned institution and individuals. What is needed today is the development of collective democratic culture within the party, its leaders, and rank and file. The collective decisions shall easily move forward to uplift the livelihoods of the people. For this to achieve, the politics transforms back as a 'service' (collective) from being a 'profession' (family) and then 'Pewa' (individual). Thus, the collective efforts shall strengthen, brighten, and gradually speed up the proactive dialogue process with India.

4. India's Soft Stands but Jingoist Mediaism

The 21st century is not a rule of the world like '-ism', and '-logy', but jingoistic mediaism. On July 14, 2020, the Darchula (local) administration of India's Uttarakhanda Province wrote a letter to Nepal's Darchula District Administration to block Nepali people from entering into Kalapani area. The official letter says, "Some Nepali groups sneak into Gunj, Kalapani, and Limpiyadhura areas illegally by crossing the border so that they draw the media attention and trouble both the local administrations" (Republica, July 27, 2020, & Singh, July 27, 2020).

Box V: Darchula, India's official letter to Nepal's Darchula District Administration to block Nepali people entering into Kalapani areas in Hindi language

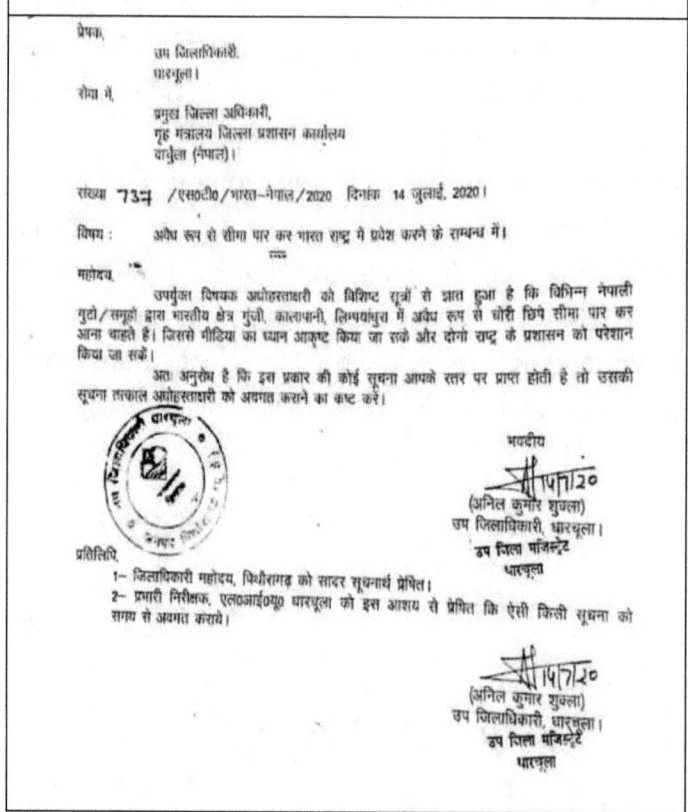

On June 13, 2020, Ministry of External Affairs spokesperson Anurag Srivastava said, "We have noted that the House of Representatives of Nepal has passed a Constitution

amendment bill for changing the map of Nepal to include parts of Indian Territory. We have already made our position clear on this matter" (The August Staff, June 18, 2020). The spokesperson of the Ministry of External Affairs, New Delhi, reiterated that the Kalapani areas belong to India without any proof, evidence, and justification.

In June 2020, former Major General Ashok K Mehta, who has an in-depth knowledge of Nepal and Nepali people, writes, "India can live with the new map, though the dissonance will harm both countries, but hit Nepal hard. The cost of ultra-nationalism will be high. The principal beneficiary will be China. The hangover of India being rebuffed over Nepal's new Constitution in 2015 and the economic blockade thereafter has not gone away" (June 26, 2020). On August 13, 2015, Mehta further said that the Lipulek Pass dispute was resolved by Maharaja Chandra Shumsher Rana and the map was handed to the British. Mehta claims "the Maharaja handed over" could be based on a case of British *force majeure* which Chandra had given sufficient inducement to accept (Cowan, December 14, 2015).

Ved Prakash Malik, a retired Chief of Staff of the Indian Army, states, "I am aware of the border problem near Lipulek Pass, which is often raised in the Nepalese media. This issue has two aspects that need to be remembered. Firstly, this is not a bilateral problem. It is a trilateral problem that involves China as well. Secondly, there has never been any problem on the ground. The people and security forces in the area have always maintained cordial relations as if there were no problem. My impression is that the issue gets articulated and highlighted in the media to obtain political publicity" (2004).

On November 12, 2008, the agreement between Foreign Minister Upendra Yadav and his counterpart Pranab Mukharjee held to resolve the Kalapani dispute bilaterally to keep China at bay. Mukharjee said, "China has already recognized Kalapani as an integral part of Nepal. India may well be trying to negate the role of China in resolving the Kalapani dispute so that it can continue its illicit presence in the area" (Border Nepal-India, 2008).

On May 16, 2020, Army Chief General M M Naravane believed that they (Nepal) might have raised the Kalapani issue at the behest of someone (Express News Service, May 16, 2020), hinting at China's possible role. Hours before Nepal's Lower House vote on a new political and administrative map, Naravane softened his voices, "We have a solid relationship with Nepal. We have geographical, cultural, historical, and religious linkages. We have very strong people-to-people connect, and that will remain strong in the future too" (Gupta, June 13, 2020).

On June 15, 2020, Senior Congress leader Karan Singh in a public statement said, "... Prime Minister Oli has moved the country into what can only be described as an irreversible confrontational posture vis-à-vis India!, despite the profound social, cultural, religious, economic, and political relations between our two countries that go back many centuries." The statement further rises, "Although the dispute in question is a long-standing one, it was, if I recall correctly, raised by Nepal in November last year. Surprisingly, we did not seem to take the matter seriously. India should have immediately initiated Foreign Secretary-level talks and then, if necessary, raised them to the level of Foreign Minister or even the Prime Ministers" (PTI, June 15, 2020). Despite Nepal's repeated request to initiative dialogues on the disputed matters, India turned deaf ear till the end of June 2022.

On June 15, 2020, addressing the cadres of Bharatiya Janata Party (BJP) in Uttarakhand, Defense Minister Rajnath Singh said, "Indo-Nepal ties are not an ordinary one. We don't have just geographical, historical or social relations with Nepal, but a spiritual one also. Who can forget Baba Pashupatinath? How can he be separated from Baba Amarnath, Somnath, and Kashi Vishwanath? If there are some misconceptions on the road between Lipulek and Dharchula among Nepal's people, then we will sit together and solve those issues through dialogue" (Das, June 15, 2020). Nothing has happened to develop talks rather than lip service to a special Nepo-India relationship.

The Indian jingoist mediaism portrayed them as the holy elephant and despised others like beetles. Explaining the baseless propaganda and insulting allegations having the relationship between, the Prime Minister of Nepal and the Chinese Ambassador cable operator, banned broadcast of those news channels starting from July 9, 2020 (The Himalayan Times, July 9, 2020). A spokesperson of the Council of Minister said, "The government holds full rights to seek remedies against those Indian media responsible for damaging the image of our country, and the nationality, sovereignty, and dignity of the Nepali people" (Giri and Neupane, July 9, 2020). Ram Khatry stated, "A large section of the Indian media is misogynist and thrives in distortion. If they are given their way, they will make "soft pornography" out of Bhagavat Gita" (July 12, 2020). Low grade misogynist media has been spreading misleading news against Nepal to increase their TRP.

Strengthening a potential controversy, Nepal's Prime Minister K.P Sharma Oli on July 13, 2020 claimed that the "real" Ayodhya lies in Nepal, not in India and that Lord Ram was born in Thori in Southern Nepal (PTI, July 14, 2020). That interpretation was received all-around criticism in Nepal. Condemning PM Oli's remarks, BJP National Spokesperson Bizay Sonkar Shastri said, "Lord Ram is a matter of faith for us, and people will not allow anybody, be it the Prime Minister of Nepal or anyone, to play with this". He further stated that the Left parties even in India played with people's faith, and the masses will reject the Communists in Nepal in the same way they have been here (Rai, July 14, 2020). Due to superior complexity and jingoistic mediaism, the numbers of communists in particular and Nepali Congress and Monarch, in general, have increased anti-Indian sentiments in them.

Veteran Congress leader Karan Singh, releasing a statement, said, "The bizarre statement by Prime Minister Oli that Lord Ram was in fact born in a village in eastern Nepal and that our Ayodhya is only an artificial concept created by India is indeed mind-boggling" (IANS, July 16, 2020). He further says, "This outrageous statement will hurt the sentiments of a billion Hindus living not only in India and Nepal but around the world" (Bhattacherjee, July 16, 2020).

India, too, has not been able to do what it should have done with its poor friendly neighbours, like Nepal. First of all, India's political intervention reached to micro-management in Nepal. While Nepal was battling a devastating Earthquake in 2015, it signed a trade and pilgrims travel agreement with China, via Lipulek Pass bypassing Nepal. History is witness that, when Nepal is in trouble, India always pursues to control its natural resources and trade for its own benefits, for instances, Koshi, Gandaki, and Mahakali, among other rivers dam agreements. Nepali people have a bitter feeling, having the implementation of the water resources Treaties signed with India, by Nepali Congress or Nepali Congress-led Government. If India's vested purpose and concern are not fulfilled, it won't hesitate to impose economic blockades similar to 1950, 1970, 1989, and 2015 again in Nepal.

Even though India is a big country, the heart of its leaders is small. It seems that the wrong policy has been taken by India to please Nepalese leaders alone without paying attention to the country and the people in general. The present territorial dispute is the foundation of ignorance to sovereign Nepal and integrity of Nepalese people. India needs to understand that Nepali people are honest and innocent unlike Nepal's leaders (in which India has purchased many of them at cheap prices) similar to leaders of Sikkim before May 1975.

The great weakness of PM Modi is that he fully trusted, depended upon, and listened to the bureaucrats-technocrats. Even Modi, similar to Nepal, has a sense of inferior complexity that educated people or scholars often hesitate to do what he is told to do. Modi has well known that such scholars focus more on how this decision can benefit the nation and the great majority of people in the long run (vision) beyond the vested interests of the Government and the ruling party. Both Modi and Oli Governments are largely depending upon bureaucrats.

Bureaucrats, as well as technocrats, often look upon personal-and-family benefits because of persistent short-sightedness, limited mindset, tactical moves, and conservative trends. Otherwise, they could advise PM Modi to not have anonymous relations with all his neighbouring states, i.e., China, Nepal, Bangladesh, and Pakistan among others. On the other, bureaucracy has a well-developed tendency of a sycophant to please the boss. If the Indian Government had appointed a scholar or wise-knowledge party leader as an Ambassador in Kathmandu, it is obvious that there would have been friendly and smooth foreign relations between two close-neighbours. Disputes or differences would be solved through meaningful (informal-formal indirect mediation or facilitation and informal-formal direct) official dialogue without delay. For this, India needs to control jingoistic propaganda which has been continued by private media for a long.

5. Negotiation by Peaceful Means

Peaceful is free from any kind of disturbance, warfare, conflict, and violence. It is untroubled by conflict and agitation, or commotion (Merriam-Webster dictionary). Peaceful is a silent protest in movement or possession. Peaceful means thinking quietly, speaking softly, writing politely, and acting together.

Negotiation is an official dialogue between two or more people/parties with a win-win or lose-lose outcome as a final result. Negotiation is an interaction between entities who aim to agree on matters of mutual interest optimizing their outcomes (Hariz, 2016). Negotiators need to use victim-centric processes to hold the negotiation maximizing mutual gains (ibid). The ultimate solution to territorial disputes is to be transformed by adopting informal and indirect (backchannel) through official/unofficial mediation and facilitation and formal and direct (front-channel) official dialogue to hold negotiations by peaceful means.

Negotiation generally occurs by familiarizing democratic and diplomatic culture of dialogue, carefully analyzing testimonies applying required technical tools to permanently resolve the Nepo-India territorial disputes. The beauty and guru mantra of liberal democracy is that any dispute or crisis must be resolved and transformed through peaceful means. For this specific purpose, it is necessary to know the history, truth, facts, figures, and testimonies that are related to the problems or conflicting issues. Apart from that, the formal arguments of the pros and cons should be collected, reviewed, observed, listened to, and analyzed carefully and collectively.

The present Nepo-India stalemate can be transformed by generating a favorable environment for dialogue to hold negotiations. Nepo-India needs to resolve or transform the territorial dispute using semi-structured and structured negotiation, adopting a process by peaceful means through proactive individuals or leadership. Peaceful means is not just about presenting evidence and testimonies between the disputing teams of both nations; it is an occasion to identify the glitches and challenges faced by each other nation and exchange and share the possible transformative ways forward for negotiation or agreement. The dialogue to hold negotiation provides a supplementary opportunity for policymakers, diplomats, think tanks, academics, and business leaders to engage in additional policy matters and ground-breaking solutions (Dahiya & Singh, 2015).

The yearning of any state party or Government is to bring or restore peace, peace dividend, tranquillity, and harmony to protect each other's nation's shared interest and desire of citizens. Just peace and harmony lie at the apex of the triangle on the Pyramid. A pyramid is a triangular based-structure of outer surfaces and sloping sides joined in a

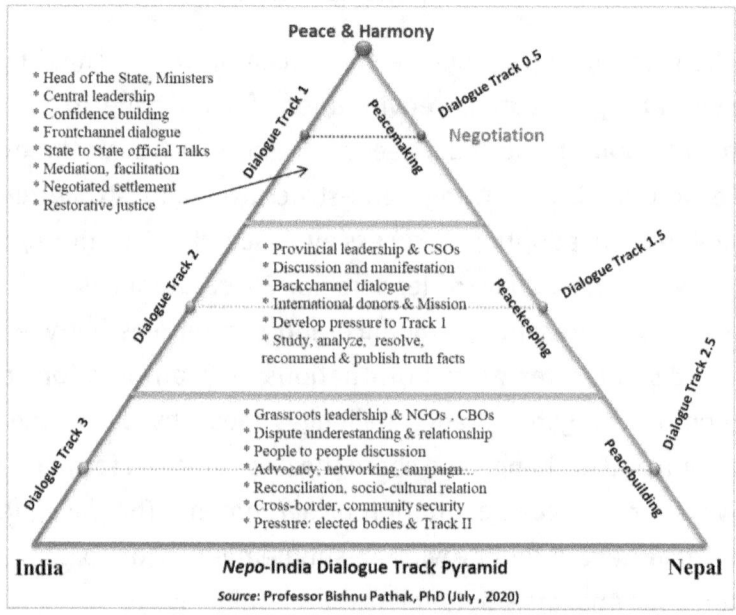

Source: Professor Bishnu Pathak, PhD (July, 2020)

point at the top (see above Triangular Pyramid). The dialogue course to hold negotiation ensures the bottom-up approach, beginning from Dialogue Tracks 3 (people to people connect at grassroots) to Track 2 (connection of regional or provincial leaders), and then Track 1 (top-most elite leaders or central leaders).

Dialogue Track 3

The Dialogue Track 3 admits people-centric (people-to-people, i.e., individuals, families, and other groups) dialogue at the grassroots. A great majority of people live in villages and communities, and spend their usual and harmonious lives from community to society. Only a small number of community leaders know what is happening in the own-and-neighboring country. All the people residing on the Nepo-India cross-border are well aware of the existing *Nepo*-India disputes and bitterness. Nepal-Indian citizens have *Roji, Roti,* and *Beti* (employment, bread, and daughter) relations for generations. There is no border wall/barrier between the nations as a demarcation line in the adjoining border; no visa is essential to and from such transnational zones. Any citizen can easily enter one another country whenever and wherever they want throughout about 2,000 km. long porous border. Cross-border people support, participate, and celebrate each other's functions even in every sorrow, festival, and happiness. People of both nations have the same food and many cases dress as well. Nepo-India has the same Sanskrit origin alphabet as the language. None of the neighboring countries has such close socio-cultural and family ties in the world. A great majority of the people and their pressure having the Nepo-India territorial disputes including Kalapani shall make a noteworthy contribution to change the present day dispute and decrease the distrust between the Governments of both nations.

Thus, Dialogue Track 3 emphasizes the peacebuilding initiatives through community dialogue, peace education, and exchanging and sharing emotions, cross-border, at grassroots levels. Such creativities need support from financial bodies such as Community-Based Organizations (CBOs), local NGOs, and local offices. Local people and community are the bases of the nation as well as political parties. Transnational people at local levels easily recognize and accept the gap between the rhetoric and truth and understand the cause of the dispute, using innocent and honest manners. The selflessness and non-ambitious nature of local people aid to transform any difficulties into peaceful means. Such people are always ready to deliver social justice to all and want to make a good history even after death through their benevolent works in their lifetime. There is no zest and zeal accomplishment of their attentiveness, rather happily and dynamically participation in peacebuilding business at the grassroots as much as possible.

Transnational people simply participate at the grassroots because of strong family and socio-cultural bonds. Such bonds tie in absolute empathy and altruism. But, they need some technical familiarity with advocacy, campaign, and networking, having territorial dispute conversion with the assistance of CBOs and NGOs. Reconciliation is a primary tool of closeness, and justice by peaceful means and changes the structural and cultural alterations or conflicts through dialogue means.

Reconciliation heals the trauma, before, during, and after the quarrel. It often involves uniting informal-formal and indirect-indirect gatherings, meetings, and conferences that generate media revelations of the disputed issues as well as politico-legal considerations at community levels.

The bulk size of Track 3 inserts the pressure at Track 2.5 to transform the Nepo-India dispute by local representatives' dialogue means. Track 2.5 belongs just above the grassroots and can have the access to hold meetings and discussions with the Dialogue Track 2 workforces, a few occasions at Track 1.5, and Track 1 too. The Track 2.5 people are normally elected representatives at the local bodies (i.e., villages and municipalities), officials, human rights activists, civil society leaders, media, institutions, mediators, teachers, and social mobilizers, among others.

Dialogue Track 2

Dialogue Track 2 aims to link a gap between Track 1 and Track 2 for a negotiated settlement, through an unarmed peacekeeping body. Track 2 accompanies the official Track 1 negotiation (Nan, 2005; Agha, Feldman, Khalidi & Schiff, 2003). The Dialogue Track 2 is known as informal, unofficial problem transformation actions aiming to develop relationships among the concerned officials or institutions inspiring a new rationale that can facilitate the official dialogue process at the horizontal-vertical tier by peaceful means. Track 2 interrelates between members of adversary groups/nations that aim to develop strategies on the course to influence public opinion and organize human and material resources in ways that help resolve their conflict (Montville, 1991).

Box-VI

Peacemaking, Peacekeeping, and Peacebuilding

Peacemaking: Peacemaking assists to facilitate the top-level of policy-making at Track 1. The policy-making body may form an informal/formal State-level dialogue team. A dialogue team is an official process of brokering peace talks and negotiations. The policy-making body has the authority to involve a third party as a facilitator or mediator. It aims to conclude dispute or violence by peaceful means. The team brings the hostile groups or disputants to a negotiated table. The negotiation ultimately concludes the dispute or violence by signing an agreement to restore peace, truth, justice, and harmony. Peacemaking reconciles the disputants if necessary. Reconciliation is a part of restorative justice and follows non-restrictive, political, diplomatic, and judicial measures.

Peacekeeping: For not to further damage or destruction to disputants, Peacekeeping monitors and enforces an agreement by force as per Track 2. Peacekeeping is an intermediary unarmed unofficial process that lies between Peacemaking (Track 1) and Peacebuilding (Track 3) to re-establish peace, justice, and harmony. Peacekeeping assists to reduce the civilian, political as well as territorial disputes by introducing informal activities for normalizing the existed situations. It presses the disputant nations to bring to the negotiating tables identifying the possible common agendas and collecting evidence and testimonies. It informally observes the entire dialogue process.

Peacebuilding: Peacebuilding is a new and broader phenomenon of a continuous process to restore a culture of justice maintaining peace and tranquility. The initiative of peacebuilding is one kind of civil society and elected bodies' involvement activities for truth-seeking/telling. Peacebuilding needs humanitarian aid to fulfill the basic needs at the Track 3 grassroots as the immediate action. It initiates before any kind of violence or dispute happens and dispute breaks out. It avoids any further loss of life. It generally identifies the causes of the violence or dispute at local levels and generates support accordingly. It prevents the recurrence of

> violence or dispute protects and promotes human security, enhances human rights, fostering livelihood, and development. Peacebuilding is a continuous process. It works at the pre-dispute phase and during the disputed triggering period. Peacemaking and Peacekeeping are parts of the Peacebuilding process (Reychler, December 2017).
>
> Source: Adapted from Nepo-India Territorial Disputes Transformation by Dialogue Means, 2021.

Track 2 influences attitude, behavior, and context of the Nepo-India disputed issue which is not a substitute for Track 1 Dialogue. It includes influential academic, religious, and civil society leaders and actors who can meet, interact, and discuss more freely the disputed issue than high-profile leaders and officials. It facilitates the Track 1 team by brainstorming the entire proceedings. Track 2 tries to provide a conducive environment for low-key, non-judgmental, non-coercive, and safe processes as needed at Track 1. It explores ideas for transformation, free from the constraints of government positions (Chigas, August 2003).

The territorial dispute is needed to discuss widely by all possible actors or institutions in order to reach a decision for a fruitful result for both sides. Nepo-India territorial dispute is a complex web of problems that need to be addressed by peaceful means by holding rigorous discussion, exchanging and sharing, reviewing the evidence and testimonies among others, and recommending it to Track I for further action. The territorial dispute is just a manifestation of the Nepo-India ineffectiveness, carelessness, ignorance, and refusal propensity of both nations to transform the dispute on time.

Track 2 is a backchannel (informal and indirect) dialogue. The backchannel dialogue inspires non-decision makers of both nations, but assists to build trust and enhancing communication. There are a lot of histories (for instance in the Middle East, French-Russian agreements on Palestine) in the world that have transformed the biggest problems by adopting backchannel dialogue.

Unofficial dialogues among the provincial leaders, academia, socio-cultural leaders, experts, and civil society leaders among others may not enough. Exchanging and sharing international experiences may need to empower them. In such *a* Nepo-India dispute, financial assistance, as well as the right experts' support, shall highly be welcomed. For this dialogue, moral international support and pressure are needed from officials including Track 1 to lessen the Nepo-India territorial dispute dialogue means.

The international community and diplomatic Mission may assist to collect relevant evidence and testimonies and may help to provide resources for study, examine the facts, find out the appropriate measures of dispute resolution and recommend their suggestions accordingly. Wide-scale dissemination of findings shall be needed to dispense to the needy officials in all Tracks in particular and people in general.

Track 1.5 belongs to the person such as a member of provincial cabinets, elected representatives, and senior level bureaucrats-technocrats. These officials shall play pivotal roles in developing pressure and assisting the measures at Track 1. Track 1.5 shall be the mainstay of dispute resolution.

Thus, Track 2 shall use large numbers of unarmed peacekeepers to empower them. The conscious citizens of both nations desire to evade any destruction of infrastructures, physical materials, and loss of life. Besides, neighborhoods and the international community may observe the dispute situation silently.

Dialogue Track 1

Dialogue Track 1 has the power to influence the negotiations and their outcomes (Sanders, 1991). Track 1 is a complement of Track 2 (Montville, 1991). Tracks 1 and 1.5 interact between official representatives of disputants which shall be mediated or facilitated by a third party (Mapendere, 2000). Mapendere says, "The aim of such interaction is to influence attitudinal changes between the parties with the objective of changing the political power structures that caused the conflict" (2000).

Track 1 is a process whereby communications of one Government go directly to the decision-making apparatus of another (Nan, June 2003). It is a formal peace process authority. The dialogue process of Track 1 transmits to Track 3 via Track 2.

Confidence-building measures are desirable to develop among the first-tier leaders of the Governments of each other nations. Such measures avoid overt hostility, minimizing fear of acceleration, interpersonal communication development, and building shared respect and trust between the nations. The snow-ball techniques and indirect-direct sharing can enhance the confidence-building measures.

In this Track 1, front-channel (formal and direct) communication officially opens a dialogue between two disputants and is visible within the protocols. The front-channel dialogue formally adopts formal diplomacy with the aim of negotiation which is to be handled by the Ministries of Foreign Affairs of both nations. The Ministries initiate Talks at various levels: joint secretaries to secretaries, and then Ministers. The neutral third party involvement assists the conflict transformation by peaceful means.

It is a voluntary process whereby a third party assists disputants to prevent, resolve or transform a conflict by helping them to develop mutually acceptable agreements (United Nations, September 2012). It is one of the effective tools for preventing, managing, and transforming disputes through voluntary means (Merrills, 2005). If *Nepo*-India identifies and uses capable persons as mediators, the resolution of territorial dispute is not that terribly difficult. Despite this, the mediator shall need to have specialized negotiation techniques, and communicative skills, and maintain neutrality.

Facilitation is a mental effort that makes the process of dialogue easy. Transformation through dialogue, active or effective participation, mutual understanding, and shared responsibility are key initiatives of facilitation. The facilitator needs to have high skills, good knowledge, structure, and process on ongoing each other nation's disputes properly (Bonner Network). Neutrality is very much important for anyone involved in the *Nepo*-India facilitation. Both facilitator and mediator may help to reduce the gap of integrative bargaining, seeking a common point.

The Dialogue Track 0.5 belongs to the Head of Government of Nepo-India, which is the uppermost government representative body of independent and sovereign nations. It is a supreme authoritative body to initiate dialogue and then hold negotiated settlements transforming territorial disputes by peaceful means. The Head of Government is an emblem of the unity and integrity of both nations inland and beyond.

Track 0.5 is the highest policy-making body. It begins formal dialogue as a matter of national, bilateral, regional, and international significance. It sets agendas, determines the issues, reconnoiters various options, examines resolutions, and ensures needed support and assistance from *Nepo-India* disputants to safeguard the voices of both nations. Such negotiated settlements shall be sustainable for truth-seeking/storytelling, peace, tranquillity, justice, and harmony endeavors. The veteran founder of peace and conflict studies, Johan Galtung, says, "By peace we mean the capacity to transform conflicts with empathy and without violence".

The last option of Track 1 is to ensure restorative justice for the normalcy of each other country's situation. Restorative justice (see Box VII) repairs the harm caused by territorial disputes. Restorative justice is initiated through reinsertion, resettlement, rehabilitation, reconciliation, reintegration, and reparation (6Rs) (Pathak, July 2020). It stresses restoring harmonious relations among people, communities, and societies in all Tracks 1, 2, and 3 of both nations.

Box-VII

6Rs of Restorative Justice

Reinsertion: Reinsertion is a short-term form of transitional support for emergency relief. It guarantees transitional assistance to the victims of flooding, landslides, conflict, and dispute among others. Reinsertion uses as the action of integrating the victims again into the society or community providing them with their immediate fundamental requirements: food, clothes, shelter, short-term education, medical services, training, employment, and so on (Pathak, 2019). This support needs for those Nepalis who often suffer in the summer seasons because of the construction of the dam, roads, and so forth by India.

Resettlement: Resettlement is an act of human compassion to find shelter in another place or nation. In general, dispute or conflict, or inundation cause displacement to the family or persons, which are being provided basic needs and other required assistance in a new location in both Nepal and India. Such settlement may be provided to the victims of border disputed areas too.

Rehabilitation: Rehabilitation includes several steps: (i) social rehabilitation, which is an act or process to rehabilitate IDPs (Internally Displaced People) in their native place, free from fear, and discrimination; (ii) psycho-social rehabilitation ensures social, educational, vocational and other forms of assistance and support; (iii) psychiatric rehabilitation restores community functioning of those individuals who suffered from psychiatric disabilities; and (iv) cognitive rehabilitation is

---

a therapy to reconnect with memories that cause the failure of personal relationships, anxiety, and trauma among others owing to dispute-induced armed conflict or natural disaster (Pathak, April-June 2013). These measures may also need to apply to the Nepali people residing in Kalapani, Limpiyadhura, Lipulek, Koshi-river victims [iv] after the construction of the bridge, and other flooding and inundation areas.

Reconciliation: Johan Galtung says that reconciliation is a process that aims at putting an end to a dispute or conflict between or among the parties (2005). He introduced 12 approaches including recovery and restitution, apology and forgiveness, judicial procedures, and punishment, karma, transitional justice, and joint sorrow. Reconciliation is a complex term (Bloomfield, October 2006). Reconciliation assists to end hostile or disputed acts and provides compensation, and healing to the victims in particular or perpetrators in general. It usually requires intervention by a third party. Large numbers of Nepali people who are now residing in disputed border areas need such healing programs to support and recover their properties lose.

Reintegration: Reintegration is a process of integrating civilian or armed forces back into the relatives, communities, and society. It is a long-term action or long-term process, which needs to be applied at local, regional, and national levels simultaneously. Because of territorial disputes in Kalapani, Lipulek, and Limpiyadhura, many Nepali citizen families are out of contact with their relatives. Once the Nepo-India dispute is settled by peaceful means, these people will get an opportunity to keep in contact with their relatives by physical means.

Reparation. Reparation is the concept of basic human rights or the principle of law. Reparation refers to making accountable the wrongdoing party (perpetrators) and compensating for the damage caused to the injured party (victims). It means, it is repairing wrongful acts (crimes) to the victims in the name of justice by the wrongdoers. Reparation provides payment both at the individual and societal levels (REDRESS, 2003). Nepali people who are living in so-claimed Indian territories and Koshi-dam, need such reparation as compensation and relief packages for their livelihoods.

Source: Adapted from Nepo-India Territorial Disputes Transformation by Dialogue Means, 2021.

As much as the suggestions of the citizens come up, the numbers of the desires and aspirations reduce, gradually shrink, and further narrow at the top of Track 1 of the Pyramid. Track 0.5 needs to ensure equal and mutual respect and benefit for territorial integrity and sovereignty, non-interference in each other nation's international and internal affairs, non-aggression, and peaceful co-existence for the sake of just peace and harmony. Thus, dispute transformation follows person to person, group to person or person to group and group to group feelings or perceptions that respect international political and legal structures and socio-cultural values and identities of each other's nations and citizens.

The basis of liberal democracy is not just to govern the state or nation winning the General Elections, but it also admits the acceptance of small nations and respect for their sovereignty, independence, integrity, autonomy, and security following the principle of Panchsheel. India must understand that, in a crisis, the (bad)-neighbor is more needed than the distant deity. Abandoning the unity of SAARC neighbors and sticking with ASEAN is sure to be a realization of a serious mistake one day for India. Everything can be changed, except the neighbors. India suffers from a risk-averting foreign policy (Bhurtel, July 1, 2020).

It is to be remarkable that India needs to encourage holding dialogue with all existing neighboring countries, including Nepal, genuinely practicing liberal democratic supremacy. For this, the formal-indirect and formal-direct dialogue techniques shall be used for the Track 1 policy-making body, and informal-indirect and informal-direct tools to be used for Track 2. Track 3 is the platform for the production of critical masses at the grassroots to exert pressure at Track 2. For formal and direct dialogues, Tracks 3, 2, and 1 are equally important for a negotiated settlement of the territorial disputes by peaceful means. Thus, the beauty of democratic culture is to resolve crises or disputes through dialogue while sitting at the table peacefully.

6. Critical Conclusions

After all, Nepal shall be victimized further even if India and China develop harmonious relations or do fight each other to prove their might is right. The giant Sino-India wants to have mutual relations and benefits through business via Lipulek Pass, neglecting the voices and suffering of the Nepalese people. Both desire to play politics to feeble neighbor Nepal.

Two different ideologies exist between India and China. India is disorderly under-governed and orderly in comparison with over-governed China. India admits bourgeois-cum competitive multi-party democracy, whereas China firmly stands on non-competitive proletarian (called) people's democracy. Proletariat politics control China's economy, whereas the economically rich people control India's politics.

Freedom is restricted in China, but starvation-famine is not heard. There is freedom in India, but famine has occurred on an empty stomach in the past. India has the highest number of beggars in the world, unlike China. The Chinese Army is completely under the control of the Government and the Party. But, sometimes, the security forces seem above the elected Government of India. Both countries have growing security interests in adopting the control theory in Nep[v] (Pathak, September 2013).

Instead, large sections of Nepalese elected bodies are under the influence of *Dalals* (brokers), *bichouliya* (middlemen), commission agents, informers, and NGOs and few of the powerful leaders have a close link with criminals in the name of their personal-family safety. In Nepal, whichever Government is formed under the leadership of anyone or party, the *dalals* and foreign spy agents encircle the Council of Ministries including the Prime Minister influencing core advisers and relatives and often controlling their duties and responsibilities. Such forces have succeeded to detach the will and aspirations of the people, wiping out the communist-and-socialist ideologies from Nepal. As a result, only nominal communist leadership exists in Nepal that has proper ideology, (political) system, policy, strategy, tactics, and practices.

In recent years, India-China struggles to increase its influence on the Government of Nepal and the party. Thus, the Government of Nepal has never completed a full five-year tenure as per the mandate of the people through General Elections in a seven decade (1950-2020) period. On the other hand, there are parties in Nepal that exist without democratic behavior, conduct, and culture and they focus more to enrich their family or courtier with money. The ruling Communist Party leader Janadarna Sharma said,

"Political sector is the center of corruption" (Onlinekhabar.com, July 26, 2020).

A large number of Nepalese people believed that Madan Kumar Bhandari (founder of the People's Multi-party Democracy) was conspiratorially assassinated in May 1993 (Amnesty International, February 14, 2000) to ratify the Integrated Mahakali Treaty owing to his strong nationalist image. Bhandari was against the Indian encroachment in Kalapani-Limpiyadhura-Lipulek (Lumsali,1997). The Secretary-General of the CPN (UML) Bhandari had led the movement against the Tanakpur Treaty signed (Bhattarai & Jain, July 4, 2015) by the then PM Girija Prasad Koirala (Nepali Congress Party) with the Indian counterpart P. V. Narasimha Rao in December 1991 (Gyawali and Dixit, March 5, 1999).

Nepo-India, as well as Indo-Sikkim treaty, was signed on the same day July 31, 1950, under the name of the Peace and Friendship Treaty (Annex – II). In the Book of *RN Kao: Gentleman Spymaster* (November 2019), the former Chief, Rameshwar Nath Kao revealed how the ruthless secret operation ran for a 27-month (December 1972-May 1975) long period that started an uprising against Sikkim's ruler (anti-Chogyal or pro-democracy movement) to annex it into India (Chauhan, December 13, 2019). Sikkim's integration into India happened while the then King Palden Thondup Namgyal 'Chogyal' of Sikkim had been pressuring India to review the Indo-Sikkim Treaty.

In December 1972, then Prime Minister Indira Gandhi asked Kao, "Can you do something about Sikkim?" (Chauhan, December 13, 2019). The merger of Sikkim with India had been a "top secret operation" in which only three RAW officers were involved (Nepal today). Kao succeeded to merge Sikkim into India on May 15, 1975. And Sikkim officially became the 22nd state of India. Before that annexation, Bangladesh was seceded from Pakistan in 1971, organizing the Liberation War in Pakistan on the secret involvement of RAW of India whose sole purpose is to 'divide and rule' all neighbors.

Kao was monitoring the King of Nepal and he concluded that the King was turning pro-China. After the Sikkim's annexation, the then PM Indira Gandhi promulgated an Emergency in the country, which was prolonged for 20 months (Nepal Today). As a result, Kao's Nepal Mission, 'if the whole of Nepal could not be annexed with India, there had been a talk of merging certain parts, mainly Tarai of Nepal' became a dilemma. The directive to annex Nepal into India stopped while the then PM India Gandhi lost her bail in the General Election 1977[vi] (Yadav, April 2014 & Online Kantipath, September 12, 2020).

If Indira Gandhi was elected, she had a plan to integrate Sikkim, Bhutan, Nepal, and Kashmir in the name of insecurity by them through India. Similar to Sikkim, Nepal has long been demanding to review, adjust, and update the 1950 Peace and Friendship Treaty. But, India argues that

Nepal is benefited more than India from the Treaty (Nayak, June 2010). Initiation of pressure not to promulgate the Republican Constitution, imposition of transit trade warfare blocking borders, inundation of entire Tarai building the dams near the border lines and construction of a road on the disputed territories among others are the common grounds of suspicion within Nepal over PM Modi whether he is heading towards the same path of Indira Gandhi, either merging whole or parts of Nepal into India.

The prolonged territorial dispute derailment neither benefits Nepal nor India. A third-party (country) shall profit from such dialogue dilemma and anonymity relations. The cohesion of mutual interest, concern and benefit are to be addressed the sooner the better. The self-realization of *sukha-dukha*, resilience, altruism, empathy, and accommodative diplomacy are today's urgency to open the knot of dialogue for a smooth negotiation process, transformation, and conclusion of disputes signing the new treaty peacefully.

Nepal is a poor, small, and weak country, but India should seriously think of about 50,000 Gorkha soldiers who have fought in favor of India in previous wars and sacrificed their lives for India's national unity, integrity, and sovereignty. Besides, China has also had some roles in this territorial dispute in Kalapani areas as the Lipulek Pass falls as a strategic tri-junction (Nepal, India, and China), but China unilaterally decided as a part of India. Therefore, the mediation of China to resolve the territorial dispute is needed.

China assists to bring Nepo-India to a dialogue table for negotiation encouraging India. History reveals that China had been silently watching the annexation of Sikkim (the then integral part of Nepal before the Sugauli Treaty) to India. Therefore, Nepal should not hesitate to hold a secret dialogue with China having the extension policy of India in its neighboring countries. India faces territorial disputes with all its neighboring countries including China as it has a lack of democratic attitude, behavior, and context in the true sense of practices.

If India wants a solution to the problem through negotiations by peaceful means, it must either expedite the submission and implementation of the EPG report or establish a high-level Territorial Dispute Resolution Committee between the two countries. Otherwise, India will continuously be without good and friendly neighbors in the entire region.

India had been liberated by the British colony long back. Even though Nepal has never been a colony of any country, it still cannot be liberated from pressure, influence, and control similar to British India. People realize that Nepal is further victimized even in the modern day as India generates pressure and control over every rank and file profession.

Annex – I : Sughauli Treaty 1816

March 4, 1816

Treaty of Peace and Friendship between the Government of Nepal and British India

Treaty of Peace between the Honourable East India Company and **Maha Rajah Bikram Sah,** Rajah of Nipal, settled between **Lieutenant-Colonel Bradshaw** on the part of the Honourable Company, in virtue of the full powers vested in him by His Excellency the Right Honourable Francis Earl of Moira Knight of the Most Noble Order of the Garter, one of His Majesty's Most Honourable Privy Council, appointed by the Court of Directors of the said Honourable Company to direct and control all affairs in the East Indies, and by Sree Gooroo Gujraj Misser and Chunder Seeker Opedeea on the part of Maha Rajah Girmaun Jode Bikran Sah Bahadur, Shumsheer Jung, in virtue of the powers to that effect vested in them by the said Rajah of Nipal, 2nd December 1815.

Whereas war has arisen between the Honourable East India Company and the Rajah of Nipal, and whereas the parties are mutually disposed to restore the relations of peace and amity which, previously to the occurrence of the late differences, had long subsisted between the two States, the following terms of peace have been agreed upon:

Article - I

There shall be perpetual peace and friendship between the Honourable East India Company and the King of Nepal.

Article - II

The Rajah of Nipal renounces all claim to the lands which were the subject of discussion between the two States before the war, and acknowledges the right of the Honourable Company to the sovereignty of those lands.

Article - III

The Rajah of Nipal hereby cedes to the Honourable the East India Company in perpetuity all the under-mentioned territories, viz-

First: – The whole of the lowlands between the Rivers Kali and Rapti.

Secondly: – The whole of the low lands (with the exception of Bootwul Khass) lying between the Rapti and the Gunduck.

Third:– The whole of the lowlands between the Gunduck and Coosah, in which the authority of the British Government has been introduced, or is in actual course of introduction.

Fourth:– All the low lands between the Rivers Mitchee and the Teestah.

Fifth:– All the territories within the hills eastward of the River Mitchee including the fort and lands of Nagree and the Pass of Nagarcote leading from Morung into the hills, together with the territory lying between that pass and nagerr. The aforesaid territory shall be evacuated by the Gurkha troops within forty days from this date.

Article - IV

With a view to indemnify the Chiefs and Barahdars of the State of Nipal, whose interests will suffer by the alienation of the lands ceded by the foregoing Article, the British Government agrees to settle pensions to the aggregate amount of two lakhs of rupees per annum on such Chiefs as may be selected by the Rajah of Nipal, and in the proportions which the Rajah may fix. As soon as the selection is made, Sunnuds shall be granted under the seal and signature of the Governor General for the pensions respectively.

Article - V

The Rajah of Nipal renounces for himself, his heirs, and successors, all claim to or connexion with the countries lying to the west of the River Kali and engages never to have any concern with those countries or the inhabitants there of.

Article - VI

The Rajah of Nipal engages never to molest to disturb the Rajah of Sikkim in the possession of his territories; but agrees, if any difference shall arise between the State of Nipal and the Rajah of Sikkim, or the subjects of either, that such differences shall be referred to the arbitration of the British Government by which award the Rajah of Nipal engages to abide.

Article - VII

The Rajah of Nipal hereby engages never to take of retain in his service any British subject, nor the subject of any European or American State, without the consent of the British Government.

Article - VIII

In order to secure and improve the relations of amity and peace hereby established between the two States, it is agreed that accredited Ministers from each shall reside at the Court of the other.

Article - IX

This treaty, consisting of nine Articles, shall be ratified by the Rajah of Nipal within fifteen days from this date, and the ratification shall be delivered to Lieutenant-Colonel Bradshaw, who engages to obtain and deliver the ratification of the Governor-General within twenty days, or sooner, if practicable. Done at Segowlee, on the 2nd day of December 1815. *PARIS BRADSHAW, Lt. Col., P.A.* Received this treaty from Chunder Seekur Opedeea, Agent on the part of the Rajah Nipal, in the valley of Muckwaunpoor, at half-past two o'clock p.m. on the 4th of March 1816, and delivered to him the Counterpart Treaty on behalf of the British Government.

Annex – II: Peace and Friendship Treaty 1950

July 31, 1950

Treaty of Peace and Friendship between the Government of India and the Government of Nepal

The Government of India and the Government of Nepal, recognising the ancient ties which have happily existed between the two countries; Desiring still further to strengthen and develop these ties and to perpetuate peace between the two countries; Have resolved therefore to enter into a Treaty of Peace and Friendship with each other, and have, for this purpose, appointed as their plenipotentiaries the following persons, namely,

1. The Government of India
    His Excellency Shri Chandreshwar Prasad Narain Singh,
    Ambassador of India in Nepal.

2. The Government of Nepal
    Mohan Shamsher Jang Bahadur Rana,
    Maharaja, Prime Minister and Supreme Commander-in-Chief of Nepal,

who having examined each other's credentials and found them good and in due form have agreed as follows:

Article 1

There shall be everlasting peace and friendship between the Government of India and the Government of Nepal. The two Governments agree mutually to acknowledge and respect the complete sovereignty, territorial integrity and independence of each other.

Article 2

The two Governments hereby undertake to inform each other of any serious friction or misunderstanding with any neighbouring State likely to cause any breach in the friendly relations subsisting between the two Governments.

Article 3

In order to establish and maintain the relations referred to in Article 1 the two Governments agree to continue diplomatic relations with each other by means of representatives with such staff as is necessary for the due performance of their functions. The representatives and such of their staff as may be agreed upon shall enjoy such diplomatic privileges and immunities as are customarily granted by international law on a reciprocal basis: Provided that in no case shall these be less than those granted to persons of a similar status of any other State having diplomatic relations with either Government.

Article 4

The two Governments agree to appoint Consuls-General, Consuls, Vice-Consuls and other consular agents, who shall reside in towns, ports and other places in each other's territory as may be agreed to. Consuls-General, Consuls, Vice-Consuls and consular agents shall be provided with exequaturs or other valid authorization of their appointment. Such exequatur or authorization is liable to be withdrawn by the country which issued it, if considered necessary. The reasons for the withdrawal shall be indicated wherever possible. The persons mentioned above shall enjoy on a reciprocal basis all the rights, privileges, exemptions and immunities that are accorded to persons of corresponding status of any other State.

Article 5

The Government of Nepal shall be free to import, from or through the territory of India, arms, ammunition or warlike material and equipment necessary for the security of Nepal. The procedure for giving effect to this arrangement shall be worked out by the two Governments acting in consultation.

Article 6

Each Government undertakes, in token of the neighbourly friendship between India and Nepal, to give to the nationals of the other, in its territory, national treatment with regard to participation in industrial and economic development of such territory and to the grant of concessions and contracts relating to such development.

Article 7

The Governments of India and Nepal agree to grant, on reciprocal basis, to the nationals of one country in the territories o the other the same privileges in the matter of residence, ownership of property, participation in trade and commerce, movement and other privileges of a similar nature.

Article 8

So far as matters dealt with herein are concerned, this Treat: cancels all previous Treaties, agreements, and engagements entered into on behalf of India between the British Government and the Government of Nepal.

Article 9

This Treaty shall come into force from the date of signature by both Governments.

Article 10

This Treaty shall remain in force until it is terminated by either party by giving one year's notice.

DONF in duplicate at Kathmandu this 31st day of July 1950.

(Signed)
CHANDRESHWAR PRASAD NARAIN SINGH
For the Government of India.

(Signed)
MOHUN SHAMSHER JANG BAHADUR RAN,
For the Government of Nepal

Annex - III: Land Revenue Receipts

Land revenue receipts of Gunji, Nabhi, and Kuti to Nepal Government until 2035 BS

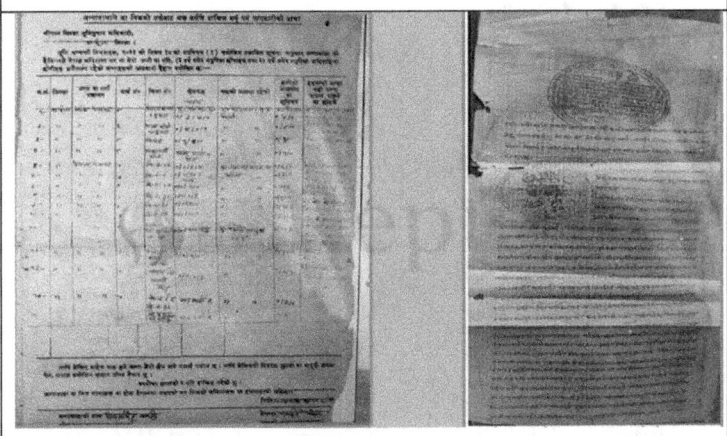

https://myrepublica.nagariknetwork.com/news/reside
nts-of-nabhi-gunji-and-kuti-used-to-pay-land-revenue-
to-nepal-until-as-early-as-2035-bs/

✳ ✳ ✳

7. References

1. Adnan, Muhamad Hariz Muhamad; Mohd Fadzil Hassan ; Izzatdin Aziz & Irving V Paputungan (2016, August). *Protocols for agent-based autonomous negotiations: A review.* DOI: 10.1109/ICCOINS.2016.7783287.

2. Agha, Hussein, Shai Feldman, Ahmad Khalidi & Zeev Schiff. (2003). *Track II Diplomacy: Lessons from the Middle East.* Cambridge: Belfer Center for Science and International Affairs.

3. Aljazeera. (2020, May 11). "Why Nepal is angry over India's new road in disputed border area". *Al Jazeera.* Doha.

4. Manzardo, Andrew E., Dahal Dilli R. & Rai, Nabin Kumar. (Undated). *The byanshi: an ethnographic note on a trading group in far western Nepal.* INAS Journal. Retrieved June 25, 2022, from himalaya.socanth.cam.ac.uk/collections/journals/contributions/pdf/INAS_03_02_06.pdf

5. Ashreuer, Christoph. (Undated). *What is a legal dispute?* Retrieved September 25, 2020, from www.univie.ac.at/intlaw/95.pdf.

6. Baral, Toya Nath. (2019, December). "Border Disputes and Its Impact on Bilateral Relation: A Case of Nepal-India International Border Management". *Journal of APF Command and Staff College.* Kathmandu.

7. Basnyat, Bonoj. (2029, November 25). "Approach to Border Encroachment". *The Kathmandu Post.* Kathmandu: Kantipur Media Group.

8.   Bhattacherjee, Kallol. (2020, July 16). "Nepali PM Oli's comment on Ram and Ayodhya 'outrageous', says former MP Karan Singh". *The Hindu*. New Delhi.

9.   Bhattarai, Binod and Rimjhim Jain. (2015, July 4). *Tanakpur treaty to come up for ratification*. Retrieved July 6, 2020, from https://www.downtoearth.org.in/news/tanakpur-treaty-to-come-up-for-ratification-30583.

10.   Bhurtel, Bhim. (2020, July 8). "Territorial nationalism a dead end for Modi". *Asian Times*.

11.   Bhusal, Jagat K. (2020, March). "Evolution of cartographic aggression by India: A study of Limpiadhura to Lipulek". *The Geographical Journal of Nepal*. Volume 13.

12.   Budhathoki, Arun. (2019, November 11). "India's Updated Political Map Sparks Controversy in Nepal". *The Diplomat*. Washington DC: Diplomat Media Inc.

13.   Bush, R. (2006). *Untying the Knot: Making Peace in the Taiwan Strait*. Brookings Institution Press.

14.   Chaudhary, Dipanjan Roy. (2020, June 1). "*India weighing response as Nepal tables bill on new map*". *The Economic Times*. New Delhi.

15.   Chauhan, Neeraj. (2019, December 13). *RN Kao: Gentlemen Spymaster*. New Delhi: Bloomsbury India.

16.   Chigas, Diana. (2003, August). *Track 2 (Citizens) Diplomacy*. Retrieved July 12, 2020, from https://www.beyondintractability.org/essay/track2_diplomacy.

17.   Conant, Eve. (2014, March 6). *Is Past Russian Meddling in Former Soviet Bloc an Omen for Crimea?* National Geographic Partners.

18. Cowan, Sam. (2015, December 14). "The Indian checkposts, Lipu Lekh, and Kalapani". *The Record*. Lalitpur.

19. Cox, J. L. (1824). *Papers regarding the administration of the Marquis Hastings in India*. London: India office Library.

20. Dahiya, Rumel & Singh, Udai Bhanu. (2015). *Delhi Dialogue VI: Realizing the ASEAN-India Vision for Partnership and Prosperity*. New Delhi: Institute for Defense Studies and Analysis.

21. Das, Kalyan. (2020, July 30). "Nepal tells India not to restrict movement of its people in contested areas in Uttarakhand". *Hindustantimes*. New Delhi.

22. Das, Kalyan. (2020, June 15). "'How can India-Nepal ties break?' In Rajnath Singh's speech references to Gorkhas and spiritual connect". *Hindustantimes*. New Delhi.

23. David, Bloomfield. (2006, October). *On Good Terms: Clarifying Reconciliation*. Berghof Research Center for Constructive Conflict Management, Berghof Report No. 14.

24. Day, Alan J. (1987, November 16). *Border and Territorial Disputes*. Keesing's Reference Publications.

25. Desh Sanchar (May 11, 2020). *Babarmahalma Andolankarile Yesari Jalaye Modi Ra Oliko Putla* (*Protestors burnt effigies of Modi and Oli at Babarmahal*). Retrieved June 30, 2020, from deshsanchar.com/2020/05/11/354249/.

26. Dhungel, Dwarika N. & Shanta B. Pun. (2009). *The India-Nepal Water Relationship Challenges*. Kathmandu: Institute for Integrated Development Studies.

27.   Dhungel, Dwarika N. & Shanta B. Pun. (2014, August). "Nepal India Relations: Territorial Border Issue with Specific Reference to Mahakali River". *Foreign Policy Research Center*. Volume 3. New Delhi.

28.   *Dispute*. Retrieved September 25, 202o from www.collinsdictionary.com/dictionary/english/disput e.

29.   Dispute.thelawdictionary. org. *What is dispute?* Retrieved September 25, 2020, from https://thelawdictionary.org/dispute/.

30.   Dixit, Kanak Mani & Tika Pd Dhakal. (2020, May 19). *Territoriality amidst Covid-19: A primer to the Lipu Lek conflict between India and Nepal*. Retrieved June 29, 2020, from https://scroll.in/article/962226/territoriality-amidst-covid-19-a-primer-to-the-lipu-lek-conflict-between-india-and-nepal.

31.   Ethirajan, Anbarasan. (2020, June 10). *India and China: How Nepal's new map is stirring old rivalries*. London: BBC News.

32.   *EurAsian Times*. (2020, July 11). "Chinese Ambassador 'Honey-Trapped' Nepal PM KP Sharma Oli – Indian Reports". New Delhi.

33.   Express News Service. (2020, May 16). "Road row: As Army Chief sees hand of third party, Nepal threatens action". *The Indian Express*. New Delhi.

34.   Galtung, Johan. (1996). *Peace by Peaceful Means*. Oslo: International Peace Research Institute.

35.   Galtung, Johan. (2000). *Conflict Transformation by Peaceful Means*. UN Disaster Management Training Programme.

36. Ghimire, Binod. (2020, June 18). "President Bhandari authenticates second amendment to the constitution". *The Kathmandu Post*. Kathmandu: Kantipur Media Group.

37. Giri, Anil & Suresh Raj Neupane. (2020, July 9). "Cable operators ban Indian news channels in response to 'insulting' video about prime minister". *The Kathmandu Post*. Kathmandu: Kantipur Media Group.

38. Giri, Anil. (2018, July 1). "EPG completes its task with single joint report". *The Kathmandu Post*. Kathmandu: Kantipur Media Group.

39. Giri, Anil. (2019, November 4). "India's new political map places disputed territory of Kalapani inside its own borders". *The Kathmandu Post*. Kathmandu: Kantipur Media Group.

40. Giri, Anil. (2020, May 10). "Nepal's Statement on Lipulek welcome, but action should follow, analysts say". *The Kathmandu Post*. Kathmandu: Kantipur Media Group.

41. Giri, Anil. (2020, May 11). "A government team consisting of Army has been quietly measuring Nepal's border with India". *The Kathmandu Post*. Kathmandu.

42. Giri, Anil. (2020, May 21). "With release of new map, Nepal and India enter a state of 'cartographic war', experts say". *The Kathmandu Post*. Kathmandu: Kantipur Media Group.

43. Giri, Anil. (2020, May 8). "India opening a road via Lipulek, a territory that Nepal claims, is a diplomatic failure". *The Kathmandu Post*. Kathmandu: The Kantipur Media Group.

44. Gundrukkhabar.com. (2020, August 25).
*Pradhanmantrika Sallahakar Dr. Bhattaraile Chiniya
Dutabasbata Paisa Liyeko Khulasa (Revealed that
money was taken from the Chinese Embassy by the
adviser Dr. Bhattarai to the Prime Minister).* Retrieved
July 25, 2020 from
https://gundrukkhabar.com/backup/18058/.

45. Gupta, Shishir. (2020, June 13). "As Nepal preps to
vote on new map, a hint about India's stance from
Army chief". *The Hindustan Times*. New Delhi.

46. Gyawali, Dipak and A. Dixit. (1999, March 5).
"Mahakali Impasse and Indo-Nepal Water Conflict".
Economic and Political Weekly. Volume, 34. Number
9.

47. Hamilton, Walter (1971). *A Geographical, Statistical,
and Historical Description of Hindostan, and the
Adjacent Countries.* Calcutta: Oriental Publishers and
Distributors.

48. Hariz, Muhamad; Adnan, Muhamad; Hassan, Mohd F.;
Aziz, Izzatdin; and Paputungan, Irving. (2016).
*Protocols for agent-based autonomous negotiations:
A review.* Kuala Lumpur.
Doi: 10.1109/ICCOINS.2016.7783287.

49. Hensel, Paul R. (2000). *Territory: Theory and Evidence
on Geography and Conflict. What Do We Know about
War?* Lanham, MD: Rowman and Littlefield.

50. Hickman, John. (2016). *Space is Power: The Seven
Rules of Territory*. London: Lexington Books.

51. Hoffmann, Steven A. (1990). *India and the China
Crisis*. Berkeley, Los Angeles and London: University of
California Press.

52. Holsti, Kalevi J. (1991). *Peace and War: Armed Conflicts and International Order, 1648–1989*. Ann Arbor: University of Michigan Press.

53. Hsin-Chi, Kuan & Maurice Brosseau. (1991). *China Review*. The Chinese University of Hong Kong: The Chinese University Press.

54. Huth, Paul K. (1996). *Standing Your Ground: Territorial Disputes and International Conflict*. Ann Arbor: University of Michigan Press.

55. IANS. (2020, July 16). *Congress Leader Karan Singh Lambasts Nepal Communist PM Oli For 'Mind-Boggling' Claim That Lord Ram Was Nepali*. Bengaluru: Kovai Media Pvt Limited.

56. Indian-Board. (1816, November 8). *The London Gazette*. Issue 1790. Whitehall.

57. *International Boundary Study*. (1965, May 30). Retrieved June 19, 2020, from https://fall.fsulawrc.com/collection/LimitsinSeas/IBSO 50.pdf.

58. Jackson, Peter. (2009, February 29). "Witness: Reporting on the Dalai Lama's escape to India". *Reuters*.

59. Jha, Hari Bansh. (2009, December 21). "Mahakali Treaty Outcome of economic nationalism". *The Himalayan Times*. Kathmandu.

60. Kafle, Parsuram and Janardan Baral. (2020, June 16). "Nepali Rastriyatamathiko Auta Dukhanta: Sadakma Janatamathi Lathicharge, Samsadma Mahakalimathi Mahaghat (A Tragedy for Nepalis: Baton Charges to the People on the Streets, Great Shocking on Mahakali in the Parliament)". *Naya Patrika*. Kathmandu: New Publication.

61. Khabarhub. (2020, May 9). *Student leaders protesting in front of Indian Embassy were arrested*. Kathmandu: Pavilion Media.

62. Khatry, Ram. (2020, July 12). *Nepalese people shouldn't hate Indian media, Indians do it for them*. SouthAsia.com.au.

63. *Long-standing border disputes between Nepal and India*. Retrieved July 27, 2020, from https://border-nepal.com/2008/11/14/long-standing-border-disputes-between-nepal-and-india/.

64. Lumsali, Rishi Raj. (1997). *Mahakali Nadibat Prapta Uplabdhiko Rakshya Gardai Thap Upalabdhikolagi Sangharsa Garau (Fight for more achievements protecting the achievements made from Mahakali River)*. Kathmandu.

65. Malik, Ved Prakash. (2004). India-Nepal Security Relations: The Challenge Ahead. New Delhi: Rupa.

66. Manandhar, Mangal Siddhi & Hriday Lal Koirala. (2001, June). "Nepal-India Boundary: River Kali as International Boundary". Tribhuvan University Journal. Volume XXIII, No. 1.

67. Manzardo, Andrew E., Dahal Dilli R. & Rai, Nabin Kumar. (Undated). The byanshi: an ethnographic note on a trading group in far western Nepal. INAS Journal. Retrieved June 25, 2022, from himalaya.socanth.cam.ac.uk/collections/journals/contributions/pdf/INAS_03_02_06.pdf

68. Mapendere, J. (2000, Summer). *Consequential Conflict Transformation Model, and the Complementarity of Track One, Track One and a Half, and Track Two Diplomacy*. The Carter Center.

69.   Masani, M.R. (1977). "India's Second Revolution".
      Journal of Asian Affairs. Volume 5, No. 1.

70.   Mehta, Ashok K. (2020, June 26). *"Why the border
      issue with Nepal flared up"*. *The Tribune*. Chandigarh.

71.   Merrills, J.G. (2005). *International Dispute Settlement*.
      Cambridge: Cambridge University Press.

72.   Ministry of Foreign Affairs. (2003, June 23).
      *Documents signed between India and China during
      Prime Minister Vajpayee's visit to China*. New Delhi:
      Government of India.

73.   Mitchell, Sara McLaughlin and Paul R. Hensel. (2010).
      "Issues and Conflict." In War: An Introduction to
      Theories and Research on Collective Violence. New
      York: Nova Science.

74.   Mitchell, Sara. (2016, May 26). *Territorial Disputes*.
      Oxford University Press.

75.   MOFA Nepal. (2020, May11). *Nepal's Foreign Ministry
      Pradeep Gyawali*. tweeted@ PradeepgyawaliK.

76.   Montville, J. (1991). "Track Two Diplomacy: The
      Arrow and the Olive Branch: A case for Track Two
      Diplomacy". *The Psychodynamics of International
      Relations*. Volume 2.

77.   Mulmi, Amish R. (2017, October 1). "Why did the
      British not colonize Nepal?" *The Record*. Retrieved
      July 7, 2020, from
      https://www.recordnepal.com/wire/features/why-
      did-the-british-not-colonize-nepal/.

78.   Mulyankan. (1999, September/October). *Kasari
      Bhayekochha Kalapanima Sima Atikraman (How the
      border is encroached in Kalapani)*. Year 17, No. 70.

79. Muni, SD. (2020, May 22). "Lipulek: The past, present and future of the Nepal-India stand-off Analysis". *The Hindustan Times*. New Delhi.

80. Nan, Susan Allen. (2003, June). *Track I Diplomacy: Beyond Intractability*. University of Colorado.

81. Napali Sansar. (2021, June 29). *Nepal-India Border Conflict Intensifies as '849 Border Pillars Go Missing' in Province* 2! Retrieved June 17, 2022, from www.nepalisansar.com/government/nepal-india-border-conflict-intensifies-as-849-border-pillars-go-missing-in-province-2/.

82. *Naya Patrika*. (2020, May 20). "Indian Army on Nepali Soil: 18 posts for 18 years". Kathmandu: New Publication.

83. Naya Pratika. (2020, May 23). *British Museum Laibrary Ra Americako Laibrary Afa Kangressma Raheko Aitihasik Naksha Bhanchha – Mahakaliko Shir Limpiyadhura (Historical maps preserved in the British Museum Library and the Library of Congress in the United States says - The Head of Mahakali is Limpiyadhura)*. Kathmandu: New Publication.

84. Nayak, Nihar R. (2015, June 9). *Controversy over Lipu-Lekh Pass: Is Nepal's Stance Politically Motivated?* New Delhi: Manohar Parrikar Institute for Defence Studies and Analysis.

85. Nayak, Nihar. (2010, June). "India-Nepal Peace and Friendship Treaty (1950): Does it Required Revision?" *Journal of Strategic Analysis*. Volume 34, Issue 4. https://doi.org/10.1080/09700161003802778.

86. Nayak, Nihar. (2012). *Nepal: Issues and Concerns in Indian-Nepal Relations*. New Delhi: Institute for Defense Studies and Analysis.

87. *Nepal-UK Relations*. Retrieved June 15, 2020 from https://uk.nepalembassy.gov.np/nepal-uk-relations/.

88. Oakley, E Sherman, (1905). *Holy Himalaya; the Religion, Traditions, and Scenery of Himalayan province (Kumaon and Garwhal)*. London: Oliphant Anderson & Ferrier.

89. Oldfield, Henry Ambrose. (1880). *Sketches of Nipal: An Essay of Nipalese Buddhism*. Volume 1. London: W.H. Allen and Co.

90. Online Kantipath. (2020, September 12). *A Scary Game of Indira Gandhi to merge Nepal into India*. Retrieved September 15, 2020, from https://www.kantipath.com/breaking-news/india-invasion-dream-of-nepal.

91. Online Khabar (2020, July 26). *Power Kendranai Bhrastcharko Kendra Ho: Sharma (Power Centers are the Center of Corruption: Sharma)*. Kathmandu. Onlinekhabar. com

92. Onlinekhabar (2020, May 10). *Pokhara students burn Modi's effigy*. Kathmandu. Onlinekhabar.com

93. Onlinekhabar (2020, May 12). *Activists including Krishna Pahadi detained for anti-India protest*. Kathmandu: Onlinekhabar.com

94. Oza, Janika. (2014, Spring). *Resisting For the River: Local Struggle Against the Proposed Saptakoshi River Dam*. Wesleyan University.

95. Pandey, Surojanga, Ramesh Sapkota & Kiran Dahal. (2020, May 26*)*. "Bartakalagi Bharat Anichhuk: Chha Jethakalagi Tayar Bhayeko Pradhanmantriestariya Telephone Barta Modile Tare (India Unwillingness to Dialogue: Modi postponed the Prime Ministerial Telephone

Conversation Scheduled for May 19(". *Naya Patrika*.
Kathmandu.

96. Parashar, Sachin. (May 19, 2020). "Boundary issue on
   bilateral agenda for two decades: Nepal". *The Times
   of India*. New Delhi.

97. Pathak, Bishnu. (2008, September 12). *The Koshi
   Deluge: A History of Disaster for Nepal*. Situation
   Update 77. Kathmandu: Peace and Conflict Studies
   Center.

98. Pathak, Bishnu. (2008, September 12). *The Koshi
   Deluge: A History of Disaster for Nepal*. Situation
   Update 77. Kathmandu: Peace and Conflict Studies
   Center.

99. Pathak, Bishnu. (2009, May 31). *Nepal-India Relations:
   Open Secret Diplomacy*. TRANSCEND Media Service.
   Retrieved May 20, 2020, from
   https://www.transcend.org/tms/2009/05/nepal-
   india-relations-open-secret-diplomacy/.

100. Pathak, Bishnu. (2013, September). "Origin and
   Development of Human Security". International
   Journal of Social and Behavioural Sciences. Volume 1,
   No. 9.

101. Pathak, Bishnu. (2014, September 15). *India's PM
   Modi towards World's Top Leader Keeping Confidence
   with Neighbours*. TRANSCEND Media Service.

102. Pathak, Bishnu. (2015). "Impacts of India's Transit
   Warfare against Nepal". *World Journal of Social
   Science Research*. Vol. 2, No. 2.

103. Pathak, Bishnu. (2019). "Transformative Harmony and
   Inharmony in Nepal's Lost Transition". *Transformative
   Harmony*. Delhi: Studera Press.

104. Paudyal, Gyanendra. (2013, July-December). "Border Dispute between Nepal and India". *Tribhuvan University Journal*, Number 35. Kathmandu.

105. Pokhrel, Krishna. (2020, May 13). "Bharatlai Bartama Lyaune Bato (The Way to Bring India into Dialogue)". *Naya Patrika*. Kathmandu: New Publication.

106. Pradhan, Tika Ram. (2020, June 29). "Faced with criticism, Oli sees plots being hatched to unseat him in Delhi and Kathmandu". *The Kathmandu Post*. Kathmandu: Kantipur Media Group.

107. Prakash, Anirudh. (2020, May 22). "I.K Gujral's misplaced altruism has lead to Kalapani dispute". *The Hills Times*. Guwahati.

108. Press Information Bureau Government of India Prime Minister's Office. (2015, May 15). *Joint Statement between the India and China during Prime Minister's visit to China*. New Delhi: Prime Minister's Office. Retrieved June 12, 2022, from pib.gov.in/newsite/printrelease.aspx?relid=121755.

109. PTI. (2020, July 14). "PM Oli says "real" Ayodhya is in Nepal and Lord Ram is Nepali; BJP rejects claim". *The Hindu*. New Delhi.

110. PTI. (2020, June 15). "'Serious diplomatic lapse': Karan Singh slams government over Indo-Nepal border row". *The New Indian Express*. New Delhi.

111. PTI. (2020, May 8). "Rajnath Singh inaugurates strategically crucial road in Uttarakhand". *The Times of India*. New Delhi.

112. Pun, Sant Bahadur. (2011). "The 1996 Mahakali Treaty: Whither the "Rashtriya Sankalpas/National Strictures" of Nepalese Parliament?" *Hydro Nepal*, Vol.11.

113. *R.K. Yadav (Former Senior R&AW Officer) Says: MQM is a powerful party in Karachi, Sindh and BBC imposed allegations that RAW is funding MQM.* Retrieved September 15, 2020, from http://www.nepaltoday.com.np/home/diplomacy_de tail?id=652.

114. Rai, Arpan. (2020, July 14). "'Lord Ram born in Nepal': PM Oli ignites new row with stunning claim on Ayodhya". *Hindustantimes*. New Delhi.

115. REDRESS. (2003). *A Source Book for Victims of Torture and Other Violations of Torture and Other Violations of Human Rights and International Humanitarian Law*. London: The REDRESS Trust.

116. Regmi, Avantika. (2019, November 29). *Lipulekako Rananitik Mahatwa (The Strategic Importance of Lipulek)*. Kathmandu: Khabarhub.com.

117. Republica. (2020, August 15). *PM Oli and his Indian counterpart Modi hold telephone conversation*. Kathmandu: Nepal Republic Media.

118. *Republica*. (2020, July 27). "India asks Darchula administration to bar Nepalis from entering India-occupied Kalapani". Kathmandu: Nepal Republic Media.

119. *Republica*. (2020, July 29). "Nepal asks Indian authorities not to bar Nepalis from entering Gunji, Kalapani and Limpiyadhura". Kathmandu: Nepal Republic Media.

120. *Republica*. (2020, June 19). "President Bhandari authenticates constitution amendment bill. Kathmandu: Nepal Republic Media.

121. *Republica*. (2020, May 16). "Indian Army chief's controversial remark on Lipu Lekh faces sharp

criticism in Nepal". Kathmandu: Nepal Republic Media.

122. Reychler, Luc. (2017, December). *Peacemaking, Peacekeeping, and Peacebuilding*. International Studies. DOI:10.1093/acrefore/9780190846626.013.274.

123. Risal, Bhairab. (2015, June 11). "I am one who has involved officially from Nepal government in collecting Census data in Limpiyadhura area in 1961". *Naya Patrika*. Kathmandu: New Publication.

124. Rose, Leo E. (1999). *Nepal and Bhutan 1988: Two Himalayan Kingdoms*. The Regents of the University of California.

125. Roy chowdhury, Adrija. (2020, June 13). "Mapping the History of Kalapani dispute between Indian and Nepal". *The Indian Express*. New Delhi.

126. Sanders, H.H. (1991). "Officials and citizens in international relations". *The Psychodynamics of International Relations*. Volume 2.

127. Santhanam, Radhika. (2019, August 12). "In Manasarovar, Chinese lend a helping hand to Indian pilgrims". *The Times of India*. New Delhi.

128. *Sardar Patel's Letter to Prime Minister Jawaharlal Nehru*. (1950, November 7). Retrieved May 22, 2020 from www.friendsoftibet.org/sardarpatel.html.

129. Scott, Bill. (1981, November 30). *The Skill of Negotiating*. Wiley, 1st Edition.

130. Shah, Dipta Prakash. (November 13, 2019). "Nepal: Sugauli Treaty-1816 & Breach of Recognized State Obligation". *Telegraphnepal*. Kathmandu.

131. Sharda, Pooja. (Undated). *Treaty of Sugauli*. Retrieved June 14, 2020 from

https://abhipedia.abhimanu.com/Article/State/NTM
wMwEEQQVVEEQQVV/Treaty-of-Sagauli-Himachal-
Pradesh-State.

132. Sharma, Bhuwan. (2020, May 30). "Residents of
Nabhi, Gunji and Kuti used to pay land revenue to
Nepal until 2035 BS". *myRepublica*. Kathmandu: Nepal
Republic Media.

133. Shrestha, Buddhi Narayan. (2003, January 1). *Border
Management of Nepal*. Kathmandu: Bhumichitra Co.

134. Shrestha, Buddhi Narayan. (2008, November). *What is
Sugauli Treaty?* Retrieved July 24, 2020, from
indiamadhesi.files.wordpress.com/2008/11/what-is-
sugauli-treaty.pdf.

135. Shrestha, Buddhi Narayan. (2010, January 17). *Border
Issues of Nepal: With Special Reference to India*.
Retrieved June 19, 2020, from
borderissuesofnepal.wordpress.com/.

136. Shrestha, Buddhi Narayan. (2015, June 22). "Yam
indeed". *The Kathmandu Post*. Kathmandu: Kantipur
Media Group.

137. Shrestha, Buddhi Narayan. (2015, June 27).
Authenticity of Lipulek border pass. Nepal Foreign
Affairs.

138. Shrestha, Buddhi Narayan. (2020, May 20). "Atikramit
Bhubhag Pauna Abako Bato (Now the Way to Get the
Encroached Territories)". *Naya Patrika*. Kathmandu:
New Publication.

139. Shrestha, Hriranya Lal. (2020, June 16).
"Matribhumiko Aastha Ra Antaraatmako Aawaj
Sunera Whip Ullanghan Garyou (We Violated the
Whip of the Party by Listening to the Voices of

Motherland's Faith and Inner Soul)". *Naya Patrika*. Kathmandu: New Publication.

140. Singh, Prakasj. (2020, July 27). "India prohibits Nepalis from entering Kalapani, Lipulek, Limpiyadhura and Gunji". *The Himalayan Times*. Kathmandu.

141. South Asia. (2020, June 29). "Nepali PM Oli Accuses Indian Embassy of Plotting to Oust Him". *The Wire*. New Delhi.

142. Starr, Harvey. (2005). "Territory, Proximity, and Spatiality: The Geography of International Conflict." *International Studies Review 7*.

143. Subedi, Ritu Raj. (Undated). "Implement The EPG Report". *The Rising Nepal*. Kathmandu.

144. Subedi, Ritu Raj. (Undated). "Revisiting Nepal-China Ties". *The Rising Nepal*. Kathmandu.

145. *Sughauli Treaty of 1815: Full Text*. Retrieved June 21, 2020, from nepaldevelopment.pbworks.com/w/page/34197552/SughauliTreatyofFullText.

146. Survey of India. (1960). *Northern frontiers of India*. New Delhi: Ministry of External Affairs, Government of India.

147. Surveyor General of India. (1961). *Political Map of India: Boundary, International: India; Nepal; others*. Sixth Edition. Published under the inspection of Colonel Rajinder Signh Kalha.

148. *Territory*. Retrieved September 25, 2020 from www.lexico.com/definition/territory.

149. *Testimony*. Retrieved September 26, 2020, from dictionary.cambridge.org/dictionary/english/testimony.

150. *Testimony*. Retrieved September 26, 2020, from www.dictionary.com/browse/testimony.

151. *Testimony*. Retrieved September 26, 2020, from www.etymonline.com/word/testimony.

152. Thakur, Prem Chandra & Krishna Kumar Sahani. (2018, July). "The Historical and Geographical Effects Treaty of Sugauli". *Multidisciplinary International Journal*. Volume 02, Number 07. Global Research Academy London.

153. Thapa, Gaurab S. (2020, May 13). "Nepal confronts India in Lipulek border dispute". *Asian Times*.

154. Thapa, Ranjit. (2010, December). *Nepal's Strategic Future: Following India, or China, or Middle Road*. Kathmandu: Tribhuvan University.

155. The August Staff. (2020, June 18). *Nepal President signs Constitution Amendment Bill for changing Nepal map*. Theaugust.com.

156. *The Economic Times*. (2020, May 15). "Nepal objected to India's road to Lipulek at someone else's behest: Army Chief". New Delhi.

157. *The Himalayan Times*. (2020, July 14). "Nepal's PM KP Sharma Oli 'claims' real Ayodhya is in Nepal: Many Remarks the Statement is in bad taste". Kathmandu: International Media Network.

158. *The Himalayan Times*. (2020, July 9). "Back Off Indian Media trends in Nepali Twittersphere, yet again". Kathmandu.

159. *The ICOW Territorial Claims Data Set*. Retrieved June 23, 2020, from www.paulhensel.org/icowterr.html.

160. *The Kathmandu Post*. (2015, June 11). "Indian Communist leader Yechury denounces India-China statement". Kathmandu: Kantipur Media Group.

161. *The Rising Nepal.* (2020, May 26). "All Party Meet For Consensus To Amend Constitution". Kathmandu: Gorkhapatra Sansthan.

162. The Wire Staff. (2020, May 11). *Nepal Foreign Minister Summons Indian Ambassador Over Lipulek Boundary Issue.* Retrieved June 25, 2020, from https://thewire.in/external-affairs/india-nepal-Lipulek-boundary-issue.

163. Toft, Monica Duffy. (2014). "Territory and War." *Journal of Peace Research 51.*

164. Tuladhar, Padma Ratna et al. (1999, September/October). *A Report Prepared by Pubic-level Border Encroachment Prevention Committee, Nepal.* Kathmandu.

165. Ujyalo Online (November 7, 2019). *Baitadima Bharatiya Pradhanmantri Narendra Modiko Putla Dahan (Effigy of Indian Prime Minister Narendra Modi was burnt at Baitadi).* Retrieved June 30, 2020, from ujyaaloonline.com/story/28532/2019/11/7/controversy-over-indias-new-political-map.

166. Wall, James A. & Michael W. Blum. (1991, June 1). "Negotiations". *Journal of Management.* doi.org/10.1177/014920639101700203.

167. Whelpton, John. (2016, June). *A History of Nepal.* Cambridge University Press.

168. Xavier, Constantino. (2020, June 11). *Interpreting the India-Nepal border dispute.* Retrieved June 7, 2020, from https://www.brookings.edu/blog/up-front/2020/06/11/interpreting-the-india-nepal-border-dispute/.

169. Yadav, R.K. (2014, April). *Mission R&AW.* Delhi: Manas Publication.

Negotiation by Peaceful Means
Nepo-India Territorial Disputes

***

Endnotes

---

[i] (1) Prof. Chaitanya Misra, (2) Bhairab Risal, (3) Prof. Om Gurung, (4) Prof. Kapil Shrestha, (5) Prof. Krishna Bhattachan, (6) Prem Bahadur Bhandari, (7) Prof. Surendra K.C., (8) Dr. Bidor Osti, (9) Dr. Baburam Bhattarai, (10) Prof. Mangal Siddhi Manandhar, (11) Chandreswar Shrestha, (12) Sindhu Nath Pyakurel, (13) Chandra Raj dhungel, (14) Maheswarman Shrestha, (15) Shyam Shrestha, (16) Pramesh Hamal, (17) Shanta Shrestha, (18) Dr. Sarad Onta, (19) Dr. Ram Man Shrestha, (20) Prof. Rajesh Gautam, (21) Ninu Chapagai, (22) Shyam Krishna Koji, (23) Buddhi Narayan Shrestha, (24) Ramesh Sharma, (25) Narayan Krishna Nhunchhe Pradhan, (26) Dr. Saroj Dhital, (27) Prof. Kalyan Dev Bhattarai, (28) Dr. Narayan Pokhrel, (29) Suresh Ale Magar, (30) Prof. Govinda Bhatta, (31) Prem Krishna Pathak, (32) Chaitanya Sharma, (33) Krishna Ram Khatri, (34) Khagendra Sangroulla, (35) Rameshwarman Amatya, (36) Jiwan Sharma, (37) Chatendra Jung Rimal Nad (38) Manik Lal Shrestha (Mulyankan, September/October 1999).

[ii] The Mahakali Treaty was signed by Nepalese Prime Minister Sher Bahadur Deuba and Indian Prime Minister P. V. Narasimha Rao in Delhi on February 12, 1996 (Jha, December 21, 2009). The Treaty was ratified by the

Parliament with a two-third majority on September 20, 1996, in Nepal (Pun, 2011).

[iii] (1) Gyanendra Shah (February 2005 to April 2006), (2) Girija Prasad Koirala (April 2006 - May 2008), (3) Puspa Kamal Dahal (August 2008 - May 2009), (4) Madhav Kumar Nepal (May 2009 - February 2011), (5) Jhal Nath Khanal (February 2011 - August 2011), (6) Dr. Baburam Bhattarai (August 2011 - March 2013), (7) Sher Bahadur Deupa (March 2013 - February 2014), (8) Sushil Koirala (February 2014 - October 2015), (9) K P Sharma Oli (October 2015 - August 2016), (10) Sher Bahadur Deuba (August 2016 - February 2018), (11) K P Oli Sharma (February 2018), and Sher Bahadur Deuba (July 2021).

[iv] Six decades (1959-63) ago when the Koshi River dam was constructed, approximately 45,000 Nepali people were displaced. In March 1956, three agendas were agreed upon: find land for affected families and the Government of India shall provide the financial assistance to build their houses as compensation; manage schools, roads, and drinking water; and provide one person employment opportunities to each family (Pathak, September 12, 2008). Sadly to say, the displaced families did get nothing. As a result, the displaced have not received justice from India to date (Oza, Spring 2014). Nor did the democratic Nepalese

Government make any effort to ensure justice for them. The government of Nepal feared that if the voices of the displaced were raised, India would angry with the Government of Nepal. History has been a witness that the Nepali people have always been humiliated by the Government of India.

[v] India tries hard to check to transfer of fake Indian currency notes and Muslim extremists and China lobbies to stop any kind of anti-Tibetan and anti-communist activities from Nepal. Besides, China is looking toward a permanent political force in Nepal similar to the erstwhile monarch in the past (Pathak, September 2013), but India desires just the opposite of it. The treaties and agreements including controlling natural resources have been compelled signed by India while Nepal has been in transition phases.

[vi] Both PM Indira Gandhi and her son Sanjay Gandhi lost their seats in the Elections as it had conducted after the end of The Emergency that had effectively suspended democracy, intimated the opposition parties, and controlled the media with authoritarian dealings (Masani, 1977).

****

About the Authors

Transnational **Professor Bishnu Pathak** was a former Senior Commissioner at the Commission of Investigation on Enforced Disappeared Persons (CIEDP), Nepal who has been a Noble Peace prize nominee 2013-2019 for his noble finding of Peace-Conflict Lifecycle similar to the ecosystem. A Board Member of the TRANSCEND Peace University holds a Ph.D. in interdisciplinary Conflict Transformation and Human Rights in about two decades. Arduous Dr. Pathak who is an author of over international paper-book publications has been used as a reference in more than 100 countries across the globe. Immense versatile personality Dr. Pathak's publications belong to Human Rights, Peace, Conflict Transformation, and Transitional Justices among others. He can be reached at ciedpnp@gmail.com.

Susmita Bastola has been completing PhD in Peace and Human Rights at Osaka Jogakuin University, Japan. Her research interest is conflict transformation, meditation, facilitation, and creating alternative mechanisms to deal with conflict and violence. She can be reached at bastolasusmita@gmail.com